The Ten
COMMANDMENTS
of SUCCESS

The Ten
COMMANDMENTS
of SUCCESS

James A. Belasco

NEW MILLENNIUM PRESS

Beverly Hills

LIBRARY OF CONGRESS CATALOGING-IN-PUBLICATION DATA
Belasco, James A.
    The ten commandments of success / James A. Belasco.
        p. cm.
    ISBN 1-893224-16-3
    1. Success in business. 2. Business ethics. I. Title.

HF5386 .B365 2000
650.1—dc21   00-029200

Printed in the United States of America

New Millennium Press
a division of NM WorldMedia, Inc.
350 S. Beverly Drive
Suite 315
Beverly Hills, California 90212

10 9 8 7 6 5 4 3 2 1

Design and composition by Sandy Bell

CONTENTS

The Ten
COMMANDMENTS
of SUCCESS

Introduction

Life is like an endless bicycle ride—lots of sweat-causing hard pedaling up hills, careful picking through crowded streets, wind-in-the-face adventures speeding down slopes, sweet-smelling meadows, and lots and lots of flat country racing. It's the Tour de France on permanent rewind.

Stop for a moment and get off the bicycle! Look around! You've been pedaling so furiously, you've hardly noticed that the scenery has changed. "What happened?" you wonder. Were you so busy pedaling head-down that you didn't notice the changes taking place?

Hmmm. Sniff the air. It smells different than you remember. There's a profusion of bright colors here, but you can't quite make out the colors or the shapes of the objects along the road. For the first time, you notice how foggy it is. You can hardly see the road ahead. You never realized how little of the road you actually can see. A panicked thought crosses your mind. "What's going on?" you wonder. "Have I lost my way?"

While you may not know where you are or what's going on, the throbbing of your muscles tells you that you'll be sore all night from the furious pedaling.

Then the competitive spirit soars within you as someone swishes past on a sleek mountain bike. You wonder, "Why is *he* doing so well? Who does he know?" Or, "How can he afford that? My own budget is stretched like a rubber band and I can't afford *that!*" These searing thoughts flash. "Am I falling behind in the race?"

Then you remember the many times, in quiet moments, that you found yourself wondering, "What's it all mean? I'm working harder than ever before, earning more money than I ever dreamed I would—and still there's this emptiness. What am I missing? What do I need? A new car? A new house? A new PalmPilot? Or is it something more than that?"

Life Is More than Toys

You've heard that the person with the most toys wins. Is that the goal? I hope not! Life is more than just another material "thing" to brag about. Perhaps you have a lot of those things already. Perhaps you've already achieved success. In the process you learned that the clock is your best friend—and your worst enemy. There's always more to do than there is time to do it.

But is life only about being busy? Been there, done that. Got the golf shirt to prove it! So what? Life is more than doing *more*—it's doing something *significant*. Making money isn't the game. Doing *meaningful* things is what it's all about.

Create Your Future

There's good news and bad news about the future. The good news is: You'll likely be successful. The bad news is: So will many of your peers.

The times have never been easier to find success—and then lose it. Although the opportunities have never been greater, the rules for capturing those opportunities have never been murkier.

"Work hard" used to be good career advice. My mom always told me that a "good worker" always had a good career. But the question is: Work hard at what? Filing? Clawing your way into a middle-management job? Plastics? The Internet? Wireless? Will any of them give you the *significance* you're looking for?

But how do you capture those ethereal opportunities? Jobs in many of these industries require a whole new set of skills. And jobs and companies in those industries seem to go in and out of fashion faster than some people change underwear. The scenery really is foggy.

A few rules do seem to apply:

✿ Prepare to outlive any organization. It'll change name, ownership, what it does, and what it needs you to do several times. Anticipate the changes and be ready for the "next big thing."

✿ Speed wins. Life more and more resembles a NASCAR race. The pace is furious on the track and changes need to be made while the car is still rolling. The standard is: Change a complete set of tires, oil, lube, and gas the vehicle in less than a minute.

✿ Flexibility is king. Learn to be a pretzel in what you do and how you think. Tomorrow will be different—in ways you can't anticipate or predict. The only way to survive is to "be like a river" and "go with the flow."

✿ Relationships are the real gold. Who you know—really know (not just to say hello)—will be the biggest asset you have. Get close to people. They will be your greatest leverage to getting where you want to go and your greatest comfort along the way.

To Grab the Future, Learn from the Past

The rules for success in the future may sound new and different. They aren't. The new economy is a lot like the old economy. There are *eternal principles*. The more things change, the more they remain the same.

Four thousand years ago at Mount Sinai, Moses brought the world the Ten Commandments. They have stood the test of time. I believe that each of us has much to learn from their timeless wisdom.

The interpretation of the Ten Commandments that follow are mine exclusively. Not being "a person of the cloth," I may have—and likely did—misinterpret or misapply the true religious meaning of the commandments. My purpose is to write a book about how to live these commandments and apply them to life in today's world—not to provide a literal interpretation of the Bible or God's word. I apologize deeply if I offend any person or any religious order as a result of what I write in the following pages.

Furthermore, it would be blasphemous for me—a mere unschooled mortal—to have the hubris to believe that I can do a better job stating the law than God Himself. It is His word that matters—not mine. I am but His humble servant. On this earth my work must be His own.

The Ten Commandments of Success can show you and me how to lead ourselves, our families, our communities, and our organizations out of the "desert" and into the "Promised Land." They lay down the way for each of us to bring success and significance, money and meaning into our lives. By embracing their timeless lessons, you will learn how to:

✵ gain control of your life, putting work, family, and community in perspective

✵ establish warm and supportive relationships with those you lead, those you follow, and those you cooperate with in your business, home, and community

✵ bring meaning and significance into your work, family, and community life

✿ be a more successful leader—and follower—at work and at home

Author Robert Fulghum put it in perspective when he wrote *All I Really Need to Know I Learned in Kindergarten*. The lessons from the past can help us grab the future.

The Basic Purpose of Life: Be the Captain of Your Fate and the Master of Your Soul

At one of those 1,000-person meetings featuring such leaders as General Colin Powell and Lady Margaret Thatcher, one of the speakers was asked, "And what is the purpose of life?" He answered quickly, "To paraphrase two lines from William Earnest Henley's poem *Invictus*, the purpose of life is 'to be the Master of My Fate, the Captain of my Soul'—and to help others become the captains of their own fates and the masters of their own souls."

Help others become the captains of their fates and the masters of their souls so they can live richer, fuller, more complete lives: that is the heart of the Ten Commandments of Success. Helping others develop elevates your own spirit. It reinforces your faith that life is more than the menial tasks you do day in and day out. You help many people achieve their destinies: those who buy from you, work with you, and live with you. It is in helping others fulfill their destinies that you achieve your higher purpose: to become the captain of your fate and the master of your soul.

These Ten Commandments provide a road map to achieving this higher purpose so that you—and others—can lead richer, fuller, and more meaningful lives.

The Ten Commandments Show You How Anybody Can Be Great

Are you ready? YES!! You're up for up, you're ready for it, and you can do it. In the following pages you will:

☼ cheer out loud when you read about Josh, the nine-year-old who couldn't hit the baseball no matter how hard he tried, who finally "got it" and hit it out of the park

☼ feel good when you read about Eric, who moves boxes in a warehouse on the midnight shift, talks to the chairman, and moves up onto the fast track

☼ feel your eyes grow misty reading about former president Jimmy Carter, who recovered from big disasters as president to become a master home builder, a chief international peace maker, and a best-selling poet

☼ want to write a check to Sister Mary Rose McGeady when you read about the "miracles" she regularly creates in helping our runaway, throwaway kids believe in themselves and establish meaningful, productive lives

There are a trillion such stories about ordinary folks—just like you and me—using these Ten Commandments and doing extraordinary things.

Okay now. Listen up! This little book will help you lift the fog and show you the road to the "Promised Land"—where the scenery is clearer, the air is fresher, and your heart is lighter. The future beckons.

Let's go!

The Ten
COMMANDMENTS
of SUCCESS

You Shall Have No Other Gods Before Me

1st Commandment

Be an Ardent Follower

I noticed him amid the chaotic hubbub of the Friday evening airport scene. He moved from seat to seat, giving a small package to everyone. When he came to my place he smiled, handed me a package with several pencils, and turned the corner to go up the next row.

The large printed insert in the package read, "My name is John. I am deaf and partially blind. I support myself by selling these pencils. Thank you for your purchase. God bless you."

How wonderful, I thought. Here's a man who chooses to work for his living rather than accept welfare or beg. I reached into my pocket to find a few dollars to buy John's pencils.

When I looked up again, John was standing in front of a very distinguished-looking woman who was examining the pencils, deciding which package to buy. She was not your average traveler. Her finely tailored clothes and graceful movements betrayed a privileged upbringing. The woman obviously didn't need the pencils John was selling.

I looked closer at her. Her face radiated a sense of peacefulness and contentment that could not be purchased with all the gold on the planet, nor captured in all the beautiful words spun by humanity's greatest poets—all for the price of a few pencils.

But who was helping whom, the leader or the follower? The gracious and obviously well-to-do woman— the leader—was helping a deaf and partially blind man earn his living. At the same time, this man was bringing the woman a peace and contentment that all her earthly possessions could never buy. In following, he led the leader to experience her noblest emotions.

The leader follows and the follower leads so that both may achieve their destinies. This is the essence of the 1st Commandment of Success.

Leaders Follow, So Others Will Follow Them

Follow those whom you help develop so you may learn how to help them become better human beings. In the process you become a better human being, too. Your ability to help others achieve their higher purpose enables them to follow you as their leader.

The Organization: Breeding Grounds for Leaders

You were taught from birth to follow people in formal leadership positions. You learned that organizations created the leaders you had to follow.

✿ In your family organization, your mother and father, older siblings, babysitters, uncles, and aunts were the leaders.

✿ In your schools, teachers, principals, and school crossing guards were your leaders.

✿ In your community, police officers, judges, and the administrators of laws—such as those concerning zoning and the environment—were leaders.

✿ At work, you learned to follow your boss and all the other bosses up the organizational ladder.

Helping Relationships Count More Than Organizational Position

Authority comes from the commitment to help others become wiser, healthier, and more capable, not from

✿

organizational position. Leadership is born out of this mutual helping relationship. I follow you because you help me achieve my destiny. You follow me so I can help you achieve your destiny.

Learn to Work Where You Don't Have the Big Organization Stick

The old organizational leadership stuff always works. Right? No, not always. Organizational leadership is useless when you're dealing with a three-party joint venture or trying to convince a hotshot Web programmer to choose to work for your organization over five competing offers.

More and More, Being "the Boss" Counts for Less and Less

My research into global leadership for the twenty-first century confirms what I hear in executive suites: *Successful leaders must be able to work effectively in nonauthority situations.*

Parents of teenagers often learn the same lesson: The formal role of parent doesn't count for much anymore.

Knowledge Is More Powerful Than Rank

Who makes the decisions that used to be made based on formal position? Once, parents decided for children and bosses decided for employees. Today it's not so simple. The truth is, the person in charge may not know enough to make the best decision. The question we should ask is, "Who knows the most about this subject?" Not, "Who's in charge?"

> ✿ Sam, a mid-level engineer for Minneapolis-Honeywell, a manufacturer of temperature controllers, led the account team for the company's largest customer. In an effort to reduce costs, the customer requested a reduction in the controller's temperature sensitivity. Sam refused the request, since granting it would mean putting an inferior product on the market. The customer called Honey-

well's president and demanded that Sam make the adjustment. Honeywell's president explained that Sam was in charge and knew the situation best. He urged the customer's engineers to work with Sam to come up with a cost-effective way to solve the problem. The story ended happily: The engineers found a win-win solution, much along the lines that Sam originally proposed.

Don't Equate the Size of the Office with the Size of the IQ or the Value of the Contribution

Is IQ like cream—rising to the top of the organizational chart? Maybe it used to be that way, but in today's knowledge-based economy, it's not necessarily that way anymore, as the following story demonstrates:

☼ Eric, a six-foot-four, 240-pound African-American male, worked part-time on the third shift in the warehouse of a large distributor. A former Marine officer who traveled in twenty-one countries, Eric is currently a paralegal who's finishing his MBA and working the third shift so his wife and three kids can have some of the "extras." He answered a general all-employee request from the chairman for business-improvement ideas. The chairman invited him to drop by for a chat, which he did. The chairman remarked, "People likely labeled Eric as a person who's only capable of doing X because of his current job title and location. Just ten minutes with Eric convinced me that he is capable of doing X, Y, and double Z. He's an articulate, well-traveled, very bright young man who wants to stay and grow with our company. He's now rapidly moving up in our organization." Smart chairman. No wonder his company is the fastest-growing Fortune 50 company and the leading company in its industry.

How do knowledge and competency create leadership? You become my leader when your knowledge and competency help me do my job, grow my soul, and achieve my higher destiny. You help me with your skills and I follow you in return. At the same time, you follow me to discover my goals so you can more effectively apply your knowledge and competency.

Be a Chameleon: Change Roles as the Needs of Your Followers Change

Learn to wear many hats—and be a quick-change artist to boot.

- ✿ Sometimes you'll wear the jaunty hat of an *individual contributor*, applying your expert knowledge to solve someone else's problem.

- ✿ Other times you'll sport the multicolored hat of the *coordinator*, helping to get diverse and often competing people to work together.

- ✿ Sometimes you'll wear the gray hat of the *spectator*, as you sit on the sidelines with nothing apparent to contribute.

- ✿ A few times you'll carry the red hat of the *decision-maker*, as others look to you for direction and finality of agreement.

Choose the hat (and your role) based upon how you maximize your contribution to others. Leadership comes from reciprocal helping relationships based upon mutual win-wins.

Find Your Followers So You Can Follow Them and Help Them Become Wiser, More Capable, and More Confident

I hear the band starting.
I must hurry to the front of the parade, for I am their leader.
—Old leadership joke

Read-the-poll politics, in which the politician reads the morning polls and decides what she's in favor of today, does not create real leaders. If you truly want to help your followers, you need to know what they need. The purpose of this entire search is: Discover others' true needs so you can more effectively fill them. In that way you become the leader that others will want to follow.

Identify those followers whom you want to understand better. These are the bosses in your life. Watch out, there are lots of these demanding folks around.

Like the Himalayan Mountains, the Big Boss Fills Your Eyeglasses

You've met the Big Boss before. There's one in every organization. Not necessarily the cigar-smoking, overweight version, but the person with a hand on the organizational hope chest of wage increases, preferred job assignments, and promotions. What's that person's definition of winning? How can you help the Big Boss win?

✿ Sometimes it's delivery of a big project.

✿ Other times it may be acknowledging the work they do. Big Bosses need appreciation, too!

✿ Often it's the unspoken words, "Don't embarrass me. Make me look good."

Fish in that pond and discover the fish food that the Big Fish needs.

Teammates and Employees Are Bigger Bosses

Teammates and employees are Bigger Bosses. They help you meet deadlines and budgets, deliver quality products or services on time, and do those thousand-and-one little extra, out-of-the-box, beyond-the-rule things that make your daily life so much easier and more productive. What do they need in order to grow and become more capable, confident, whole human beings?

✿ Many folks want to learn new skills.

✿ Most people want to know what's expected of them and how they're doing.

✿ Almost everyone wants control over his or her immediate work environment—not curing world hunger, but fixing the water fountain that doesn't work.

✿ Everyone wants to be treated with *respect* for his or her ideas and for who he/she is.

Each person's definition of these "must-haves" is different, so you need to do pretty extensive fieldwork to discover Sam's needs as they differ from Judy's.

Customers Are Another Bigger Boss

Who buys what you produce? You may work as a programmer, secretary, planner, analyst, manager, or small business owner. Whatever job you have, you're making something for someone who will use what you produce to make his or her life easier, better, more productive, more satisfying, and happier. Follow them so you can find out:

☼ who they are

☼ what they value in what you produce

☼ which problems or issues they face—now and in the future—that you might help them solve

Follow your customers to find out how you can help them be better people by using what you deliver.

Family—The Even Bigger Bosses

Families are the Even Bigger Bosses. Family members often get overlooked, but they are significant players in your life. Forget following them to discover their needs to be better people and you guarantee that you will be an outsider among your inner circle.

☼ Your spouse looks for valuable emotions, such as respect, affection, and intimacy—pretty important ingredients in a relationship.

☼ Your children want admiration and applause. You'd like some of that back yourself, I'd wager.

☼ Your parents want to be proud of you so they can brag to their buddies about your achievements and accomplishments. You'll be in their shoes one day looking for the same thing from your kids.

Follow your family members to ensure that blood remains thicker than water and that you have a safe haven filled with folks who really care about you.

Regardless of which boss you follow at any given time—organizational, teammate, customer, or family member— the purpose is always the same:

Find out how you can help them be wiser, more capable, and more confident of their abilities so they can function more on their own and fulfill their destiny. Then they will be willing to follow you.

APPLICATION

Who are your most important bosses?

_____
_____
_____
_____
_____
_____
_____
_____
_____

How can you best help them fulfill their destinies?

_____
_____
_____
_____
_____
_____
_____
_____
_____
_____
_____
_____
_____
_____
_____

Get Your Ph.D. in Followership

You've probably never taken a formal program in followership, but here's the slimmed-down, primer, crash course in how to be a more effective follower. It's a no-brainer!

Get a Mental Lobotomy to Remove That Old Leadership Picture

I've had to do the equivalent of a frontal lobotomy in order to become a more effective follower of those whom I wanted to follow me. The biggest obstacle I encountered was my own mental picture of my role as a leader. For years I saw myself as the answer man, chief decision-maker, and principal asset allocator. Upon reflection, I was such a micro-manager that I wouldn't even work for myself—and lots of people chose not to. My business limped along, regardless of the long hours I put in.

Get Clear on Your Destiny

Learn to replace that "me-the-controller" picture with a more other-centered, growth-oriented one. See your job in the following ways:

Deliver Great Performance to All of Your Bosses

This grows their souls and yours. Encourage people to take on tough jobs—and help ordinary Clark Kents become Supermen. Follow them closely, discover what they need to reach the next level of performance, and work hard to help them get what they need to succeed.

Admit You Don't Know and Ask for Help

As much as you may hate to admit it, you can't know everything about everything. There's a lot that you don't know—
and you need other people's input to help you. It may be
hard for you to say the words "I don't know" when someone
asks you a question. It's an art to know when to request help.
Do it too soon and you look like a wimp. Wait too long and
you become a loser. It's hard to learn, but you can get better
at it.

> ✿ A machinist I know struggled for several days to pro-
> duce a part to repair a jet plane. Try as he might, he
> couldn't get it right. He asked me what he should do.
> "Ask the master mechanic," I suggested. "But won't
> that look like I don't know my job?" he asked. I
> responded, "Do you think that making the wrong
> part and having the plane ditch in the ocean is a bet-
> ter alternative to asking for help?" Reluctantly, he
> went to work the next day and asked for help. When I
> saw him later, he was smiling from ear to ear. "The
> master mechanic told me that no one's been able to
> figure out how to make that part, and that I made the
> most progress in figuring out how to do it," he said.
> "Thanks, that was great advice." Most people I know
> would prefer a request for help in advance rather
> than an explanation of the error afterward.

Get the Needed Resources and Remove the Obstacles to Your Bosses' Success

One of your major tasks is to identify the obstacles that prevent your bosses from achieving their goals—and then working with your bosses to remove them. Whether it's buying a
new file cabinet, a car for your teenager, or modifying the
company's compensation system, help your bosses achieve
their goals by removing the impediments in their path.

So What's Followership Got to Do with My Life, Anyway?

That's a legitimate question. After all, what I'm proposing seems to fly in the face of much that you've learned in classrooms and experienced in life. The old hierarchical model is well established in our collective consciousness. Just because it's there, though, doesn't mean that it's right—or useful.

Ponder a few questions with me:

✷ What gives you a kick in life? Is it watching your kid score the winning touchdown? Is it seeing your child deliver the commencement address? Is it your company team winning the Malcolm Baldridge Award? The basic point is: For many folks (myself included), it brings great pleasure to see those near and dear to them win.

✷ Beyond all the fancy cars, big houses, and expensive trips, what brings you real joy? I mean deep-in-your-soul, down-to-the-bottom-of-your-toes, capital letters J-O-Y. I'm reminded of the words of my dear friend Ralph Stayer: "My greatest joy is in watching people grow." Amen, friend.

So, here's the top and bottom line of the 1st Commandment:

Make a difference in your world—and bring real meaning into your life.

- Follow those you lead by developing an other-oriented, help-people-grow mentality.

- Learn how to help people become wiser, more capable, and more confident than they might have been had you not been their follower-leader.

All of which gives you the opportunity to fulfill your own destiny.

You Shall Not Make for Yourself
an Idol

2ndCommandment

Reflect Humility

For twenty-two years he served as chairman of his company. He built a single plumbing business into one of the largest conglomerates in the world. His face adorned the cover of every leading business magazine. He lunched and dined with presidents and kings. His management techniques formed the basis for entire courses at the master's level in major universities.

But age and fashion extracted its price. The chairman's health waned at about the same time that conglomerates like his went out of style on Wall Street. The chorus of hoorays turned into a constant harangue urging him to sell off major pieces of his empire. Earnings kept growing, but the stock price dove.

The chairman evaluated the situation and made his decision. At the next board meeting—to the surprise of everyone, including his closest confidants—he announced that he no longer had the heart or the energy to disassemble all that he'd spent a lifetime building and had decided to retire from his position as chairman. He urged the board to appoint a search committee find a new chairman with the vision and energy to lead the company in its new direction.

The chairman put the needs of others—his stockholders, employees, customers, and community—ahead of his own. He lived the essence of the 2nd Commandment of Success: Reflect humility in your thoughts and actions.

Beware the Distractions

They pulsate like Las Vegas billboards calling out to you: fast cars, alcohol- and drug-induced highs, fancy clothes, big houses, *Business Week* cover stories, an office overlooking the skyline, private jets, fawning minions. The neon lights are everywhere. These are today's idols. Many of us energetically pursue these modern-day images of money, success, and fame. Some of us allow that pursuit to turn our heads from our *real* task: helping others become wiser, more capable, and more confident in order to become the captains of their fates and the masters of their souls.

It's not success that spoils people; it's how that success was achieved. There are lots of distractions out there to turn your head and divert you. It's easy to fall into the "money pit" or the "sex pit" or the "power pit." The idols call to you all the time.

Idols distract us from our primary focus of helping others. Hubris, arrogance, and ego are the ultimate idols. Putting others first—whether they're customers, employees, family members, or community members—and helping them become finer people requires a humbleness and humility of spirit and action. Humility speaks of the "we," not the "I," looks to pass on the credit for accomplishments, and steps forward to willingly accept blame for errors.

Think for a minute about the people you enjoy being with. I don't know about you, but I really like to be around people who share the limelight, pass on credit, and take their share of the blame. I feel a lot more comfortable around people whom I know I can count on to support me in my efforts. In my work or play, I seek out those who look for the good things about me and ignore the rest. I search for folks who help me feel better about myself when I'm with them. These are the people who live the message of the 2nd

Commandment of Success. They are treasured friends, team-mates, and family members.

Learn humility and you will find meaning and significance beyond your wildest dreams. That's what the 2nd Commandment of Success is all about.

Put Others First

It seems as if the world revolves around "I, I, I." Listen to the number of sentences that begin with the personal pronoun "I"—or are sprinkled with it liberally—throughout a conversation. Listen to your own sentences—and be shocked at the prominence of "I." A sister of one of my business friends, commenting on her brother, remarked, "Listening to him you'd think he was an only child." Such behavior reeks of self-centeredness, the antithesis of the 2nd Commandment.

See Yourself as the Vehicle for Others' Growth and Enrichment

"But," you ask, "how can I reconcile commitment to my career and putting others first?" "How can you not?" is my simple reply. It all begins with the attitude of the person in the mirror. Let's begin there.

✿ President Jimmy Carter was one of many one-term presidents in the second half of the twentieth century. Historians generally agree that he was not a strong president. After completing his term he could have crept back to his home in Georgia, nursed his wounds, grown his peanuts, and faded from the public eye. Instead, he followed his heart and his values and focused on helping others grow into finer human beings. His work—bringing peace to several troubled parts of the world—will likely write his name in the history books in larger letters than his record as president. President Carter used his leadership experience to help others become more capable, competent, and whole human beings. In doing so he ensured his place in history.

☼ I work with the owners and stockholders of a privately held company that seeks to operate in accordance with the biblical Ten Commandments. After many debates over a mission statement, the owners and stockholders decided that "work that satisfies the soul of the person doing it, the person receiving it, and the person financially benefiting from it" fulfills the injunctions of the Ten Commandments. Specifically, they agreed upon the following: work that fulfills the deepest desires and needs of associates and employees; products, services, and experiences that delight their receivers (customers, suppliers, community members); and financial results that exceed those that could be realized from other similar business ventures.

The organization enjoys an enviable record in delighting customers and growing associates while delivering extraordinary financial returns. It just might be that the company's not-so-secret secret is its focus on using the Ten Commandments to serve its employees, customers, suppliers, communities, and stockholders—creating one whale of a successful business.

Get Passionate about Helping Others Grow Their Souls

"Put everything you've got into anything you do," Zig Ziglar intones from the platform. Halfway measures usually produce no-way results. Life without passion isn't life at all—it's "near life." So to paraphrase a once-popular song, "You gotta have passion, miles and miles and miles of passion." But it has to be passion with the "right" purpose—and in this context the right purpose is one that puts others first and helps them lead richer and more productive lives.

> ✿ Tom Moran, president and CEO of Mutual of America, a $10 billion insurance firm, told employees in a comment initially made by William Flynn, former president and CEO and now chairman of the board: "The day we have to downsize, the day we have to eliminate jobs, my name will be first on the list." Talk about passion for helping others!

Passion for Work

Passion for work is both an idol and a blessing. Many folks become workaholics, forgoing family, vacations, and community life for hours in the office or on the road. You've met many of these people in your business travels. They are usually sharp-edged, aggressive individuals who can quote you the number of widgets sold in Peoria last week but can't recall their daughter's birthday.

However, passion for work can also provide the opportunity to grow others—as well as yield rich material rewards for you.

> ✿ Neighbor Tom worked eight days a week. He was passionately committed to his work—and to the people who worked with him. He talked incessantly about "his job" and "his people." He'd forever bring interns home for dinner and invite secretaries and their families over to swim in the pool on weekends. He devoted a great deal of energy to a local teenage drug rehabilitation facility, often inviting everyone over to barbecue and swim on hot summer days. Although Tom worked hard at his job, he worked equally hard at developing people. Tom retired with

enough in his 401(k) to buy his dream home in the Florida Keys, where he fishes much of the year. Hard work was a blessing for Tom, and he used that hard work to help others.

Beware False Passions

Watch out for the truly deadly idols: alcohol, tobacco, food, drugs, and sex. Your senses are constantly assaulted with messages in the media telling you that smoking is cool, drinking is in, eating is a lot is fun, and sex is okay anywhere, anytime, and with anybody.

But there's a big difference between social drinking and alcoholism. According to many doctors, a glass of wine at dinner helps prevent heart attacks. A little wine may be a good thing. But for some people, alcohol takes over their lives. They become addicts, searching for the next drink, the next fix, the next high. Be careful, a little wine may be a good thing; a lot of wine may become a very bad thing.

The same is true about eating, smoking, and recreational sex. A good meal that satisfies the appetite is a pleasure. A big meal may place an undue strain on your heart and cause long-term medical problems. Similarly, uncontrolled sex drives have ruined many company stars.

☼ Imagine yourself in a far-off city on a business trip. It's late and you're in the bar unwinding after a hard meeting. A particularly attractive colleague of the opposite sex sits down next to you and subtly but clearly indicates an interest in being intimate with you. You've been happily married for some time. What do you do? You're flattered. Your hormones send you one message, your conscience another. Your choice will speak volumes about your true passions.

Learn this basic message: Avoid activities that do not afford the opportunities to put others first and help you help them lead fuller lives; they easily become idols that distract you.

✿

**Get passionate
about helping others
grow their ability
to become the captains
of their fate
and the masters
of their souls.**

Share the Glory, Be Willing to Take the Blame

Avoid the Ugly Cast of Nonsharing Characters

There are people who hog the limelight. They are real pains to be around. They're the first to grab the chalk to make the presentation (especially if the Big Boss is in the audience). Worse, their self-centered behavior prevents other folks from growing their skills.

Another real "winner" is the person who's always right. You've met these smart alecks, I bet. They glory in recounting in great detail all the times they were "right" about decisions, even when someone else (typically a higher-up) didn't listen to them and made the "wrong" decision. Their favorite phrases are, "I told you so. If they'd only listened to me . . . " They cut off discussion, kill innovation, and destroy motivation. Real winners, aren't they?

Fill Your Play with the "Good Guys" Who Share the Stage

These antihumility types display just the opposite message of the 2nd Commandment. Many people we know relish sharing the glory. They realize that they can't succeed without their teammates. Sharing the credit helps to encourage additional contribution. It's a lot more fun and a whole lot more productive to work and live with folks who share the spotlight. Everyone learns. Everyone grows. Everyone benefits. Talk about win-win-win.

Step Up to the Table and Accept Your Share of the Blame

Don't you just love all those "big shots" who suddenly disappear when a program goes sour? As the saying goes, "Success has many fathers, but failure is an orphan." I've personally experienced too many of these situations and have been a participant in at least a few of them.

✼ Early in my career I was the manager of the production department at a manufacturing plant. It seemed that we always had short lead times and that the production tooling department was the biggest obstacle to meeting our goals. The situation between the two departments eventually broke out into open warfare. "All's fair in love and war," I thought at the time. This was clearly war, so my youthful enthusiasm drove me to win at all costs. We hatched a scheme to discredit the production tooling department's work. We kept careful records of promised versus actual delivery dates, planned versus actual tool performance, and days of production lost due to the department's failure to deliver. We posted big charts in the production area and I buried my boss in a blizzard of paper pointing out the department's deficiencies. Three months into the campaign, my boss gave me control of the department and transferred the current department head to another plant. In the production department we exalted over our victory.

It was not my most shining hour. I am deeply ashamed of what I did. I did not step up to the table and take my share of the blame for the production shortfalls. Rather than examining how I might have improved my department's performance, I focused instead on proving that someone else was wrong. Worse, I passed up an opportunity to learn. My future performance suffered as a result.

You Are Not Your Position. Don't Wear Your Robes to Bed.

Too many folks I know cannot separate the person they are from the position they occupy.

   ✿ A school superintendent I worked with many years
ago personified this difficulty. He talked only about
policy. He spent his time in his office holding meetings with his immediate staff. In eleven years I never
knew him to visit a classroom, speak with a student,
dialogue with a parent, exchange ideas with a teacher,
or engage in discussion with a community member.
He wore his suit to the supermarket and the barber
("You have to always look the part," he said). Even at
our frequent Saturday meetings, he was formally
dressed.

Keep clear that who and what you are is different from the position you hold in any organization. In addition to being a father, with certain parental responsibilities, I am also a sixty-three-year-old male with a certain personality. I may be the president of my company, but in addition I am a husband to my wife, who is not an employee of my company. I ignore that distinction at my own peril.

"Father Knows Best" Has Been Canceled and Is No Longer in Reruns

I know many people who are impressed with their "title." I used to be one myself. But I learned the hard way that this doesn't work when my twenty-three-year-old son cussed me out during his wedding rehearsal, stomped off, and told me to either "butt out or get out." I was forced to admit that my always-having-a-better-answer-than-anybody attitude threat-ened to ruin my son's wedding and our relationship. Then and there I swore that my primary task from that day on would be to help my son develop his own abilities, rather than tell him what I thought was best for him.

I realized that the best judgment of a parent's ability is how the child lives his or her adult life. If the child crashes and burns upon coming of age, give that parent an F for doing a poor parenting job. If, on the other hand, the child-turned-adult prospers and improves, give that person an A for outstanding parenting performance.

After all, how do you really want to be remembered? Do you want your tombstone to repeat all the job titles you've held (assuming that your heirs could get them all on your headstone)? I can't speak for you, but I know for myself I want to be remembered more for what I've helped others become than for the jobs I've held.

**Share the glory.
Take the blame.**

APPLICATION

What one action can you take to share the glory?

_____
_____
_____
_____
_____
_____
_____
_____
_____
_____

What one action can you take to accept the blame?

_____
_____
_____
_____
_____
_____
_____
_____
_____
_____
_____
_____
_____
_____
_____
_____

You Shall Not Misuse
the Name of the Lord Thy God

Grace and Honor Others with Your Words

She's earned an M.D. and a Ph.D. from two prestigious institutions. She's president of a start-up company looking for venture capital funding. This is her third start-up.

Her clients were due at 2:00 P.M. At 2:05 P.M., three male venture capitalists hurry through the door, the senior partner at the head of the phalanx. He quickly looks around, takes off his coat, hands it to her, and says, "Here, girl, please tell Dr. Smyth that we're here. Oh, and I'd like some coffee, black with one sugar, please."

She hangs up the man's coat, goes into the kitchen, gets him the coffee he requested, returns, and offers it to him with the words, "Here you are, boy, Dr. Smyth at your service."

"Maybe it was his guilt or something. But it was the easiest seven million dollars we ever raised," Dr. Smyth told me.

With his words, the male venture capitalist dishonored the very person he was seeking to sell. He forgot that his words were the messengers of his soul, reflecting his true beliefs and character. He violated the 3rd Commandment of Success, which urges you to grace and honor others with your words and enable them to grow to become greater people. Use your words to honor and grace others, thus helping you soar. This is the essence of the 3rd Commandment.

Your Words Paint a Picture:
Be Sure It's a Rembrandt

Your language can help others grow their souls and become finer people. A billboard I saw recently says it all: "My second name is not DAM. (Signed) God." Words paint a picture. They tell a story. They create a reality. Listen to and feel the difference between the words "girl" and "woman." One projects a picture of an immature, dependent, female child. The other paints a picture of a mature, self-sufficient female. Which word do you think Dr. Smyth preferred?

Words Reflect What You Think about Others and Create an Image of Them

I remember my mother always talking about her "no-good, lazy Uncle Sam." To me, Uncle Sam seemed like a nice, easy-going guy. I could never figure out why my mother didn't like him. He always had a nickel or a dime for me, so I sort of liked him. However, I never trusted him because of what my mother called him.

Many years later, after he had passed on, I asked my mother about Uncle Sam and why she called him lazy and no good. Seems that he bet horse races for a living. To my mother, betting was not a legitimate profession. She thought only lowlifes and crooks hung out at the racetrack. When I asked her how well he did, she was hesitant to answer. "He must have cheated a lot," she said. "I don't know exactly, but Aunt Sue [his wife] had a fur coat, and they drove a fancy car and had a summer place in the mountains." To the end, my mother could not bring herself to admit that betting was a legitimate occupation. Her words reflected her view of my Uncle Sam and created an unflattering picture of him in my mind.

Words Can Dishonor Others

In too many discussions, words are fired like machine-gun bullets, designed to dishonor and disable the other person.

✪ We've all sat in staff meetings that have degenerated into shouting matches and name-calling brawls. At one meeting of the senior management staff of a mid-sized foundry company, the words got so heavy that several folks actually left the meeting. That didn't stop the combatants from continuing their verbal assaults on one another. The fact that the owner was one of the participants helped to contribute to the vituperative outpouring.

✪ Do you recall the movie *Who's Afraid of Virginia Woolf?*, starring Elizabeth Taylor and Richard Burton? In that movie the two protagonists use their words to embarrass, defame, and destroy both their guests and each other. They are masters in the use of words, and they use their mastery to skewer one another and anyone else on the scene. That movie represents what the 3rd Commandment urges you to guard against.

With the words "Let it be," God created heaven and earth. With your words you create your heaven and your earth—and your hell. Words are powerful creators of your reality. Choose them carefully.

Speak *Only* Those Words You Truly Mean

Words spoken in jest sometimes reveal more than we want them to. Two personal experiences illustrate this point.

✪ I was shocked at what I'd just heard. We were lounging in the clubroom of a very expensive golf club in California, swapping airplane-travel war stories. One of us, the CEO of a Fortune 50 company, piped up, "I've sat next to all kinds of weirdos in my day, but last week took the cake. I was traveling from Denver to Newark and the guy next to me just smelled up the place. I mean body odor that I couldn't believe. I spent most of the trip walking around the plane because I couldn't stand to sit in my seat. But what do you expect from a nigger?" Some of the other guys laughed. I could not believe my ears. Here it was, the year 2000, and I was sitting next to a man who was widely recognized as a leader in equal opportunity employment, but who was, in fact, a closet racist.

✿ My first summer college internship was with a large company in New York City. I was thrilled to get the job. During my first month, I traveled with several executives to the company's facility in Lancaster, Pennsylvania. The plant manager of the facility invited us to meet at his house for drinks one night prior to going out for dinner. He asked me about my background, education, and what I wanted to do when I graduated. I was prepared for these "employment"-type questions. Then he asked me about my religious background. He was visibly shaken when I told him. He quickly added, "Oh, some of my best friends are . . ." and changed the subject.

The rest of the internship was uneventful. At the end of the summer we shook hands, said goodbye, and that was that. I was disappointed that the company never offered me a permanent position. Many years later I encountered one of the executives at a seminar. During our conversation I shared with him my disappointment at not having received an offer of permanent employment. He looked furtively around and, lowering his voice, said, "Well, to tell you the truth—and it's long enough in the past that I feel okay in telling it you—we'd never hired anyone before from your religion. We had heard all these stories about people like you and we just were not sure. So we decided that you looked okay, but we couldn't take the chance."

My summer employment was in 1956 and that final conversation was in 1978. I didn't feel bad about what the man said. That was just the way things were back then. But my recent experience with racism makes me wonder how much real progress we've made.

Offhand Comments Often Reveal Not-So-Offhand Feelings

Words create labels. We've talked about the labeling impact of words like "girl" as opposed to "woman." But what about the impact of words used to describe different ethnic groups, like "spic" or "Hebe" or "wetback"? They also create labels. Using such words may seem harmless, but remember, every word implants a picture. Use words that grace and honor, not denigrate, others.

> ✿ Ethnic jokes perpetuate labels, creating attitudes among people of an entire culture. I've heard the same joke told in many places with different ethnic targets: Asians, Irish, and Polish. The Dutch, for instance, make jokes about the Belgian people. One popular joke goes like this: "The dumbest man in Holland just moved to Belgium—and raised the IQ in both countries." It always gets a laugh in Amsterdam and a boo in Brussels. What does that joke say, though, about how the Dutch view the Belgians? Could some of the distrust displayed by Dutch politicians toward the European Union bureaucracy be based upon its location in Belgium?

Your Words Create Your Reality

Words are powerful messages. They shape reality—yours and others'. You can't help it. You are a role model to others in your life.

✿ I once worked with a twist drill manufacturing company. Brent, the owner, was a brilliant businessman. He designed the tools and did most of the marketing. He loved his design activities and dealing with customers, but he had a very low opinion of his production workers. Brent's attitude showed—in his words and in his and his managers' behaviors. They disrespected employees, called them "assholes" and "stupid," and looked for ways to control them. They even instituted random daily personal searches to make certain that employees weren't stealing the twist drills.

The employees, in turn, lived up to the expectation. They worked hard to not work hard. For example, rather than look for a missing process spec sheet, they'd ask their supervisor to get it for them, even if it took hours. Turnover was a big problem. Quality was another.

Several years later I ran into Brent. He'd sold the twist drill business following a disastrous strike. "I'm now in the machine tool design business. I have a small group of designers working with me; they're just wonderful people. I'm having a ball—and making more money than I've ever made in my life. You once told me something like 'give people expectations to reach for, not labels to live down.' I took those words to heart. Giving people high expectations to reach for, and encouraging them to keep reaching, has paid off in spades for me."

Brent learned a valuable lesson—and the price was very reasonable: Your words create your reality. Use profane and irreverent words about others, dishonoring them, and you create a reality in which they act in profane and dishonoring ways toward you.

The opposite also works:

- Sister Mary Rose McGeady teaches the neediest of the needy to believe in themselves. You'll find her Covenant House's national "Nine Line," 800-999-9999, scrawled on the walls of places you don't want to go. Sister Mary Rose offers hope to the lost young people of our world. She reaches them through her outreach vans, which roam the back alleys frequented by young runaways and throwaways, and at her shelters in ten U.S. cities.

  Her goal: Do whatever it takes to get these young people to believe in themselves, start down the road to recovery, and begin to lead meaningful, productive lives. She first reprograms their language. No drug talk or loser talk is allowed. She gets them to talk instead about spiritual values, finding jobs, living healthy lives. "As long as you're with Sister Mary Rose, and working your program, you're a winner," she teaches.

I believe in Sister Mary Rose because I've seen miraculous recoveries by addicts who learn to talk a different language—a language that reflects positively on how they feel about themselves and the other people with whom they live and work. I've seen sixteen-year-olds who've done every drug imaginable (and some you can't imagine) and beat-up, worn-down sixty-six-year-olds come back from the living dead to lead honest, productive, meaningful lives.

Let your words:

- enrich the receiver

- be the ambassadors from your caring heart and worthy soul

- bring the grace and honor that blesses both the receiver and the sender

Acknowledge the Contributions of Others

N o one makes it alone in today's world. Even the Lone Ranger didn't ride alone: he had Tonto. Charles Lindbergh, the Lone Eagle, had a whole team back at Ryan Aircraft Company in San Diego support-ing him and his effort to fly that first transatlantic flight to Paris. Each of us has a huge team behind us. How can you honor and grace those wonderful people who help you per-form your important work? The simple answer is: Acknowl-edge their contributions.

Acknowledgment Is a Personal Process

E-mail is an increasingly popular way to keep lots of people informed about activities. Voice mail is a wondrous commu-nications tool. But when it comes to acknowledgment, there is no substitute for face-to-face contact. Words delivered in person always carry greater weight than words delivered almost any other way.

> ✿ When Sam Walton was alive, he frequently brought coffee and doughnuts at 2 A.M. on the day preceding the grand opening of one of his WalMart stores. He did it to show his personal appreciation for those folks who were working extra hard to make the open-ing a success. He was the richest man in America, yet he took the time to personally thank the folks who were working through the night. No wonder he was so successful.

✹ When Jack Welch was a newly minted CEO at General Electric, he launched a program to reduce costs on purchased parts. He installed a special red phone in his office and asked purchasing agents across the company to call him anytime they reduced the cost of a product. Welch answered the phone whenever it rang—even interrupting meetings—to personally thank the individual for his or her efforts. He then dashed off a handwritten note, thanking the person again. As a demonstration of the power of personal acknowledgment, many of those notes still hang, framed, on the walls of the company.

✹ Following the suggestion of Kenneth Blanchard, coauthor of *The One Minute Manager*, Neil Stratton, a police captain in Walnut Creek, California, awards "champion cards" whenever he catches someone doing something right. This has been so effective for the police department that other city jurisdictions have adopted the technique.

Acknowledgment benefits both the receiver and the giver. The receiver is honored to receive the contributions of others toward the achievement of his or her goals. The giver is honored by the acknowledgment of the value of his or her contribution. Both are honored and graced by mutual respect. Grace and honor others with your words, for in that exchange you also grace and honor yourself.

Take the time to
acknowledge another's
contribution to you.
Personal
acknowledgment is the
ultimate gratification
for you both.

APPLICATION

List one person's contribution to you.

_____

_____

_____

_____

_____

_____

_____

_____

_____

_____

Create one Rembrandt with your words about another person.

_____

_____

_____

_____

_____

_____

_____

_____

_____

_____

_____

_____

_____

_____

_____

_____

Remember the Sabbath Day by Keeping It Holy

4TH COMMANDMENT

Always Be a Student

He founded and leads a successful manufacturing company whose stock rocketed from three dollars a share to over forty dollars in less than six years. Copies of high-profile Forbes *and* Business Week *articles on him and his company paper his walls. By any financial standard, he is very successful.*

I had answered his call for a "few minutes of conversation." It is Tuesday afternoon at 2 P.M., and he is out with his twelve-year-old son playing basketball. On Thursday, he and his ten-year-old daughter leave for a four-day father-daughter retreat. Two weeks from now he will go with the entire family for a week of river rafting. Will his stockholders be up in arms? After all, he's playing hooky, being with his children rather than looking after their business. It is likely they won't. Their returns are in the top 10 percent of all publicly traded companies over that six-year period. Maybe they should encourage him to slip away more often.

"I need time for reflection and gaining perspective. The job is too fast paced and demanding not to take that time," he said.

This executive understands the need for time off from the job to do well on the job. He is following the 4th Commandment of Success: Take the time to learn—about yourself and your higher purpose.

Learn Your Lessons Well

To reach your higher purpose—to truly become the captain of your fate and the master of your soul, and help others do the same—you need time to work "on" yourself. That's why the 4th Commandment of the Bible urges you to remember the Sabbath and keep it holy.

The Sabbath was about rest and restoration of body and soul. It was a time when the entire family and community studied, worshipped, and recommitted themselves individually and collectively to their spiritual quest. The Sabbath helped renew their faith. In that context, holy meant set apart.

The 4th Commandment of Success also urges you to set aside "holy" time—to work "on" yourself and renew, reflect, and rededicate yourself to your higher purpose.

Mistakes Are Great Teachers

Have you ever been called upon to give an answer in front of a Very Important Group (especially one filled with Bosses, Big Bosses, and Even Bigger Bosses) and not know what to say? It has happened to most of us. Mistakes are not fatal and we do learn from them.

> ✿ A large consumer goods manufacturer did extraordinarily well in the 1980s. Until around 1988 it was the talk of the market: the top revenue line grew at 20-plus percent every year, with good margins and increasing stock prices. Then the bottom fell out. Both the consumer market and the stock market went south, and the easy financing money dried up. The company ended up with millions of dollars in unsold inventory. The top line flattened out and the bottom line fell into the red zone. That's about when I appeared to work with the chairman.

"We got blind-sided by the market," he explained to the board. One board member asked pointedly, "Why weren't you ready for this tough stretch? The tax law change in 1985 presaged this drying up in the financing market, didn't it?" The chairman stumbled through some answer, but felt afterward that he'd made a grievous mistake and had looked bad in front of the board.

How could he recover? He took an entire day with his executive team, focusing on what they learned from this mistake and how they could avoid it in the future. Out of that meeting evolved an early-warning information system that the chairman shared every quarter with the board. He was ready for the next economic earthquake. In just a few years, he was chosen his industry's Executive of the Year—nominated by that same questioning board member. The chairman learned from his mistake and became a better leader as a result.

Mistakes Are Life's Trial by Fire: Are You Ready to Walk across the Hot Coals?

Mistakes give you the opportunity to test whether you're really serious about your words. Life is not a straight shot up. Rather, it's a series of midcourse corrections. In fact, the Apollo moon shots were "off course" more than 90 percent of the time.

> ✿ Carol, a small business owner, had her own rite of passage. Her dress shop specialized in petite sizes. Her first shop did so well that she opened several others. Running her business like a one-woman band proved to be her Waterloo. She handled everything—from leasing, merchandising, and hiring to advertising. As she was getting ready to open her fifth

store, she placed her $400,000 opening merchandise order and, as usual, waited until the last minute to ship it. Just when the store was due to open she received a panic call from her secretary: The bank refused the $400,000 financing and the manufacturer refused to ship. It seems Carol was overextended on her credit line. Simply put, she was out of money. She was so busy opening stores that no one was watching the cash. Forced to eat a large helping of crow, Carol sold two stores. Now, much wiser, she's got a chain of stores—and a strong chief financial officer to track the cash.

Mistakes are great teachers. Make original mistakes only.

APPLICATION

What was the biggest mistake you made this month?

_____

_____

_____

_____

_____

_____

_____

_____

What did you learn from it, and how will you apply what
you've learned?

_____

_____

_____

_____

_____

_____

_____

_____

_____

_____

_____

_____

_____

Learning Is a Personal Contact Sport: No Spectators Allowed

L earning doesn't happen *to* you; it happens *through* you. You are not an empty vessel that some teacher fills with learning. You must be an actor on the stage, completely immersed in the play of your life, not a spectator in the second row. Learning is scary and takes a strong dedication. Like learning to ski, you fall down a lot, look foolish, and come down the bunny slope on your rear end. All of those embarrassments—and insults to your "I'm-a-success" image—are the necessary steps to schussing and cutting down the slope.

Beware the "I'm-Too-Busy" Trap

Many people I know talk about wanting a better-paying job, more education, or a brighter future. Not all, however, truly dedicate the time and energy to learn what it takes to grow their skills and competencies.

✵ Farouk was a graduate student at a fine business school. He was admitted because he convinced the admissions committee that he really wanted to learn how to make a major difference in his native country. He regularly asked his professors about business opportunities that might be developed in his country, but he never took the time to learn about any one opportunity in depth. He was always rushing off to do "something important." He left school before the end of his final term, pleading that he had "important work to do back in his country," and promising to return within a year.

Years later, a curious and concerned counselor contacted Farouk in his country and was told that he was "very busy" working on his family's farm. Farouk told the counselor that he planned to come back "someday soon" and finish his degree so he could learn more about business opportunities that he might explore in his country.

Farouk was "too busy" for a Sabbath that would help him become the captain of his fate and the master of his soul.

Escape the "Success" Trap

It's easy to get comfortable with your success. You've made it, so why spend all that time learning something different? The answer is very simple: If you don't, you'll disappear. The world changes so rapidly these days that if you don't learn new things, new ways, and new approaches, your sun will set and you will be history.

The Future Belongs to the Learner—Not the Learned

Like most things in our Internet-driven world, learning has a very short shelf life. I thought I had learned the "truth" in undergraduate school—only to discover that when I returned seven years later for an advanced degree, most of what I knew to be true just wasn't so anymore. Given the rapid decay rate for learning, you just have to keep at it. Being learned means that you know yesterday's way. Being a learner means that you are discovering tomorrow's way. Which do you think takes you into the future?

Dollars Belong to the Learners

People with high school diplomas make double the earnings of those who left before they graduated. Those with college degrees make five times the lifetime earnings of high school graduates. Learning is one of the best investments in your future you can make.

Learning Begins with That Person in the Mirror—and a Hurt That Won't Quit

Learning begins with a deep, abiding commitment to be different. It starts in the soul and percolates throughout your life.

- An executive I know knew his business wasn't going as well as he wanted. He tried many new approaches to engage his people in the business, all of which failed. He turned over his executive team twice in two years as people quit, frustrated because of his constantly changing "programs." I got his attention one day with the startling statement, "My friend, *you* are the problem." "Can't be," he replied defensively. I convinced him to record a staff meeting. The tape devastated him. He cut people off, swallowed their sentences, raised his voice when they disagreed, and didn't listen to anyone else's ideas. "I've got to change," he said. That fateful tape began a several-year journey during which my friend learned new ways of dealing with people. He turned his business around, grew it many times over, was chosen Executive of the Year by several leading publications, and launched a new life of charitable work.

- When I decided to return to the university to earn my Ph.D., I had no idea how I was going to do that or where that step might lead me. I just knew that I had to escape my current situation. Not that my situation was bad. It was actually very good. I ran a manufacturing plant, had a consulting business on the side, and was active in several other business ventures. But the knot in my stomach just wouldn't go away. I needed fulfillment. I couldn't verbalize it or rationalize it; I just knew I had to go and do it. That "Sabbath" changed my life in ways I could never have anticipated or planned.

Show Up on the Field Where the Learning Takes Place

Learning is applied doing. You learn best from doing. So find opportunities to do—and then make certain that you learn from the doing.

✿ Kurt was a very talented design engineer at a large oil refining company. He wanted to learn more about hydrogen-based fuel cells so he could become an expert in designing the manufacturing facilities to produce them. He believed that hydrogen fuel cells would become a large portion of the current hydro-carbon gasoline market, so he wanted to be ready when that happened. He proposed a six-month leave of absence to study hydrogen fuel cell technology and its manufacture.

Today he leads the company's fuel cell program, reporting directly to the board of directors. One of the directors told me, "Kurt's an amazing person. He did it all on his own. When he came to us with his proposal, he was so passionate about it that it was impossible to turn him down. Don't quote me on it, but he's got the inside track to head up our fuel cell activity once it reaches critical mass stage."

✿ Maria Montessori theorized that children learn best when they are actively engaged in playfully manipu-lating shapes, objects, and words. She turned her theory into an opportunity and developed the suc-cessful Montessori program.

✹ Today's academics have a new toy to test their theories about how kids learn best: the Internet. Idit Harel developed her theory of "constructionism" while earning her Ph.D. at MIT. She believed that kids learn best while actively involved in creating things rather than just passively sitting in their seats listening to a lecture. To test her theory—and make a little money in today's "dot-com" world—she founded MaMaMedia, a "kinetic kaleidoscope that allows children to build their own homepages, create cartoon identities, play games, and surf prescreened educational sites to the beat of a bouncy sound track."

Job assignments are wonderful learn-by-doing opportunities, though they aren't the only ones. Relationships and family experiences also offer great learning opportunities. Try raising children and see what you learn.

Around every corner is another learning opportunity. Seize those precious moments.

Build In Learning Time

Most likely you're so busy "doing"—rushing from project to project, meeting to meeting—that you never have the time to learn from all your doing. You need a "Sabbath" at the end of every meeting, every project, every day to reflect upon what you've learned and how you can use that learning to do better next time. Try some of these ideas:

✹ Practice the "ten-minute rule." For every hour of a meeting, take ten minutes to identify the things you learned that can help you be more effective in the next meeting. Focus first on learning about the process—how you work together, how the meeting was structured, and how you used (or misused) meeting facilitation tools. Then explore what you learned about the content.

☼ Set learning objectives for every meeting. Ask people at the end of every meeting, "What did you learn from this meeting and how will you use it?"

☼ Make it a practice to stop folks in the hallways and ask, "What did you learn this week and how are you going to apply it?"

☼ Cut out items from newspapers, journals, and magazines and send them to others to stimulate their continuous learning.

Many of these "learning time" suggestions apply in your personal life as well. For example, ask your children, "What did you learn this week and how will you apply it?" You—and they—will be surprised at the quality of the discussion that follows (after they get over the initial shock of your question).

I find that asking seat mates on airplanes, "What's the most surprising thing you've learned this year?" often leads to deep, personal conversations—and friendships that grow over the years.

Build the Girders and Beams of Your Learning System

In theory, everyone's in favor of learning, yet we leave it mostly to chance. Here are some ways to build a system that automatically reinforces the learning mentality:

☼ Set annual learning objectives and work on them weekly. Everyone has his or her own "to do" list—just be certain that you also have a "to learn" list. Inspect and measure your learning frequently.

☼ Set both personal and career learning objectives. You are more than the job you do, and your interests go beyond learning how to type faster or design aircraft parts better. Set personal learning objectives, like learning a language, or understanding your kids better, or taking up line dancing. Learning is for life.

✹ Meet with other learners. Get together with other folks who are dedicated to learning. Swap ideas and learn how to learn from one another. I used to hold monthly lunches with a small group of folks I admired and respected. Some people called it a "mastermind" group. I paid for the lunches. From the great ideas I picked up and the energy and motivation I got just from hanging out with them, I figured I got the price of the lunch back many times over.

The key message of the 4th Commandment of Success is: Observe your "Sabbath" and keep it holy. Take a "Sabbath" time to work *on* your life as well as *in* your life. Observe a "Sabbath" time every day to learn how to grow captaining and mastery skills.

> **Keep your inner school always in session. Observe and keep holy the "Sabbath" of learning and rededication to your higher purpose.**

Honor Your Father and Your Mother

5TH COMMANDMENT

Honor Your Relationships

"I flew thirty-seven successful missions off the deck of the carrier in Vietnam. My thirty-eighth mission was not so successful. I was shot down, captured, and spent five and a half years as a prisoner of war before being released in the armistice.

"Several years later a man approached me in a hotel lobby. 'Hi, Commander, how have you been?' he asked. Seems we served on the same carrier in the Gulf.

"After exchanging pleasantries, I asked, 'What did you do on board, sailor?'

"'Packed chutes,' he replied.

"'How'd you like the job?' I asked.

"'Not bad, and it kept me out of harm's way,' he said.

"We chatted for a while longer about old times and then said goodbye. On the way home that evening I realized that I probably owed my life to that man. He likely packed my chute, which opened perfectly that fateful morning and enabled me to land safely. I owed my life to that man, and I never even knew him or thanked him.

"Then I realized that my life is filled with people who 'pack my chute'—my family chute, my career chute, my community chute, my financial chute. From that day forward I promised to identify and acknowledge all the 'chute packers' in my life."

—A FORMER NAVY PILOT

We Are All Family

We are family," the song tells us. "And we pack each other's chute," the navy pilot's story reminds us. The 5th Commandment of Success imprints this interdependence on our soul.

Most commandments of the Bible warn us to avoid bad things—swearing, murdering, committing adultery, stealing. Only two urge us to take a specific positive action: the 4th Commandment—to observe the Sabbath and keep it holy—and the 5th Commandment—to honor your father and mother.

"Be a Learner," the 4th Commandment of Success urges, so we can grow and become wiser, more competent, more capable, and more confident. This is the intellectual dimension of life: growing your head. "Honor Your Family," the 5th Commandment of Success intones, so you can experience the caring and support so central to a fulfilling life. This is the emotional dimension: growing your heart. You need to grow both your head and your heart if you are to be the captain of your fate and the master of your soul and help others to become the same.

Family is the model for all relationships—whether a primary family, a work group/team family, or the family of all humankind. Family is a relationship based upon mutual caring and support, which lies at the heart of all human relationships. The best way we honor members of a family is to help them grow and enrich their lives.

Recognize the Intricate Web of "Family" Members

You have many members of a family with whom you are connected: some you know, most you don't. You have many connections: some you know, most you don't. Start with all those people at work—teammates in your department, your site,

✦

and your company. Then add the whole cast of characters you reach through the companies of your customers and suppliers. You are also connected to other folks in your industry, with whom you compete sometimes and cooperate other times. Don't forget all of those personal connections that fill up your PalmPilot or Day-Timer: high school chums or college alumni, fellow professionals, local officials, and neighbors. Of course, you can't forget your primary family: mother, father, sister, brother, spouse, and children. And then there's the extended family, reaching into third and fourth cousins, several times removed. That adds up to several thousand connections that are part of your "family"—and that doesn't begin to count all those faceless and nameless members of your humankind family. These "family" connections form the stage and props you use to star in the movie called *My Wonderful Life*.

We Need Other "Family" Members to Survive and Thrive

"The knee bone's connected to the thigh bone. The thigh bone's connected to the hip bone, the hip bone's connected to the back bone . . . Now hear the word of the Lord," the old spiritual goes. We're all connected—and because of that we all need each other. Fingers need hands that need bodies. Healthy fingers and hands depend upon a healthy person. A healthy person depends upon a healthy community, a healthy nation, and a healthy planet. So my health depends upon your health. My success, therefore, depends upon your success. In a biological sense I must be as committed to helping you succeed as I am to helping myself succeed. Isn't that logical? Of course.

Can "Little Old Me" Make a Difference?

There are so many members of your "family" that it's easy to
feel powerless. It's easy to wonder, "After all, how much difference can one person make?" Actually, you'd be amazed at
the difference individuals have made throughout history—and
we're talking about ordinary folks like you and me, not kings
and presidents.

☼ James C. Bulin was a very ordinary guy who spent his
   life as one of an army of designers forever putting
   lines on paper at Ford Motor Company. He was
   always looking at designs in a different way, which
   made him very unpopular with his colleagues. In its
   July 29, 1996, issue, however, *Business Week* reported
   that Ford executives singled out Bulin for his contribution to the success of Ford's best-selling F-150
   truck. It seems that Bulin was so concerned about
   creating success for the members of his customer
   family that he turned the standard design process on
   its ear. Rather than looking first at other successful
   cars, Bulin focused on customers' desires. He
   identified different generations and their values and
   tastes—and then suggested designs for each group.
   One ordinary person contributed well over $1 billion
   to Ford's coffers.

☼ Thanks to Michael Slaughter, a very ordinary minis-
   ter, the Ginghamsburg United Methodist Church,
   once a ninety-person congregation in a minuscule
   Ohio village, grew to more than two thousand in little more than ten years. Once a small country
   church, Ginghamsburg is now a sprawling, bustling
   campus that includes a large community church
   building, a resale clothing store, a women's counsel-
   ing center, a food pantry, a community-crisis outreach facility, a furniture warehouse, three children's

clubhouses, and four educational buildings. The church rocks the entire weekend with activities and four separate worship services aimed at different segments of the church's membership. Attendance averages over three thousand each weekend.

In his book *Spiritual Entrepreneurs: Six Principles for Risking Renewal,* Slaughter underplays his role in the expansion. Rather, he praises the power of small "family" groups who incorporate others with similar interests into their "family." These small groups (or cells) "have the power to break addictions, overcome co-dependent tendencies, and restore broken relationships." They also provide the key to soul growth for both the giver and receiver.

Look out over the mosaic of your "family." Find ways to help its members grow to become better, richer, more fulfilled individuals—people who are more capable and competent in growing themselves and helping others grow as well.

Be the instrument for your family members becoming better, richer, more fulfilled individuals.

Treat Everyone as Family

O n our way to lunch across the carefully manicured grounds, a CEO of a very large company and I encountered a maintenance supervisor yelling at a groundskeeper. The CEO stopped some distance away and waited until the supervisor finished and started to walk away. "Got a minute, John?" he called over. The slightly embarrassed supervisor hustled over to where we were standing. After some bantering, the CEO asked the supervisor, "John, would you talk to your mother that way?" "Of course not," the supervisor replied, "but if I don't make the point strong enough this guy just won't pay attention. Besides, this is business and we've got to get the work done." The CEO urged John to think about some other ways to get the employee's attention, and we continued on our way.

"We won't get much work done around here with that kind of attitude," the CEO said, shaking his head sadly. "I keep talking about our need to bring people together. It'll never work as long as supervisors like John keep treating people like third-class citizens."

Treat employees, customers, suppliers, community members, and stockholders as you would a member of your family—because they are!

Share the Pie—and Watch It Grow

My mother made the best icebox pie in the world: layers of whipped cream and crushed graham crackers. Yum, yum. We kids all fought to get the largest piece. Finally, she hit upon a way to resolve our squabbling. One of us would cut the pie and the others choose the slice—and whoever helped prepare the pie got to choose first. All three of us soon learned that the key to getting more pie to eat was to help prepare a larger pie so that each slice could be bigger. My mother taught me an important lesson: Sharing the pie with all those who helped create it makes a bigger pie for everyone.

✻ Kingston Technology is a large manufacturer of add-on memory modules for PCs. The business is based upon the owners' Asian family values, which include paying above-average wages and offering a very generous profit-sharing plan. The company also treats suppliers and customers as "members of the family." It does business the old-fashioned way, without big contracts and lawyers, but based on a handshake and trust. Kingston pays before it has to and never cancels an order because supplies are tight. A deal is a deal. In the components business, that's a very big benefit to customers and suppliers.

Because Kingston shares the pie, the company keeps growing. Sales double every year. Revenues top $800 million. And sales per employee are more than eight times greater than the nearest competitor. According to a 1994 article in *The Economist*, the overhead is the lowest in the business, and the company turns over its inventory an unheard-of three times a day!

Grow a bigger pie by sharing it with your "family."

Treat Others—Employees, Customers, Suppliers, Community Members—As You Would Your Father and Your Mother

The CEO's question—"Would you talk to your mother that way?"—gets right to the point: Treat everyone with the respect and caring that characterize family relationships. When negotiating with a supplier, ask yourself: "Would I deal with my father this way?" When deciding whether to take a certain action involving the community in which you live and work, ask yourself: "Would I do this to my mother's house?" These are powerful questions that force us to think about our treatment of others and ask whether it really ennobles them and helps them experience success.

✪ A long time ago, I managed a manufacturing plant that generated lots of contaminated waste water. We ran the waste water through our septic and leach field system, as there wasn't any public sewer in our vicinity. While the practice was perfectly legal then, I was wrong in handling contaminated waste in that manner. I absolutely never would have done it if I had first asked myself the question, "Would I do this to my mother's house?"

✪ Sam and Joan bought a small lot in our area. In an effort to expand their lot to meet the minimum requirements for lot sizes, they attempted to buy small pieces of adjoining lots. Neighbor John had an all-glass house and had planted thick bushes and trees in the rear of his lot for privacy. He agreed to sell a piece of his back lot to Sam and Joan, providing they didn't build on it. Sam and Joan assured John that they also wanted to preserve the wooded privacy barrier.

Soon after the closing, much to John's chagrin,

Sam and Joan cleared the wooded area and turned it into a playground. John complained loudly, but Sam said, "Look, we changed our minds. The property is ours to do with what we want now. Sorry." John was very unhappy.

About a year later, Sam and Joan discovered that they were two feet short of the minimum setback requirements and needed each neighbor to agree to waive the zoning requirement. John absolutely refused. Sam and Joan were forced to move their house. Not treating John with the caring and respect of a family member cost them thousands of dollars.

Put Family First—They, and You, Deserve It

Do you feel that there's no time for your family? Then there's something clearly out of balance. Time is the magic ingredient in every successful, caring, respectful, supportive family relationship. How you spend your time speaks volumes about your priorities. If family isn't one of them, it will show up in the absence of your family members from your agenda book. Make time to be with your family, particularly your primary family. It's a soul-satisfying experience.

> ✿ Leonard D. Schaeffer, chairman and CEO of Cali-fornia-based Wellpoint Health Network, learned about the importance of family early in his child-rearing days. He was working hard, climbing the lad-der of the federal bureaucracy, when he faced a conflict: His daughter's kindergarten play and an important meeting were scheduled at the same time. Being the typical driven, upwardly mobile executive, Schaeffer planned to skip the play and attend the meeting. His wife wouldn't hear of it. She won. He went to the play and was the only dad there. He says,

"My daughter still talks about it to this day. I think it's one of the reasons she became an actress."

That started a precedent. He attended every one of his daughter's performances and every one of his son's athletic events. Schaeffer says, "Once I arrived by helicopter. Once, in a tuxedo. But I went to every one." Schaeffer demonstrated with his time that he cared for his family.

Your mother is alive and well—and living inside every person with whom you deal. Your father is thriving and prosperous—and exists deep within every business or commercial interaction you experience. See their faces and hear their constant admonitions.

You Are Your Brother's Keeper and Your ...

The rhetorical question is frequently asked, "Am I to be my brother's keeper?" The 5th Commandment of Success answers uncompromisingly, "Yes! And your neighbor's keeper and your customer's keeper and your teammate's keeper, and your you-name-it's keeper. In fact, we are each keepers of the other, because we are all family, and as family we look out for, care for, and support each other."

✿ My wife sent me a card one Valentine's Day that said, "Thanks for seeing the good in me and overlooking the rest." No wonder I love her so much.

Family members look for the good in other family members, encourage them to succeed, and respect their ideas, judgments, and decisions. That is the test of true family caring and support—and the essence of the 5th Commandment.

Treat those in your
community, your work,
and your social circles
as you would treat your
father and mother.

APPLICATION

List one situation in which you will treat an employee or a
coworker as you would treat your mother.

_____

_____

_____

_____

_____

_____

_____

_____

List one situation in which you will treat a customer or a
neighbor as you would treat your father.

_____

_____

_____

_____

_____

_____

_____

_____

_____

_____

You Shall Not Murder

Be the Instrument
for Others' Soul Growth

Actor James Caan took a sabbatical at the height of his career—fresh from an Academy Award nomination for The Godfather. Instead of acting, he took up coaching kids sports. He particularly remembers one nine-year-old named Josh. Josh was big, but he just couldn't hit a baseball, and it really bothered him. Caan spent many one-on-one hours coaching Josh.

As Caan tells it, "The next to the last game of the year Josh comes up to bat. The week before he had popped it up to the pitcher with the bases loaded. He felt terrible. Anyway, he gets up, and he just creams the ball. And the kid starts running. I'm coaching third base, and he looks up at me when he rounds second. When he saw me waving him on to home, he looks at me—I'll never forget it as long as I live—and there were tears in his eyes. He ran home, jumped up in the air, and landed with both feet on the plate. He triumphantly pumped both fists in the air. The whole dugout cleared out to hug him. Nothing replaces that. Nothing in the world. I mean, to literally change a kid. That was the best time of my life."

The 6th Commandment of Success is about helping others—like the Joshes of the world—experience the kind of fulfillment they thought they'd never have.

Be the Vehicle/Coach for Others' Development

Murder occurs in many ways. There's physical murder, of course, which robs the person of life. More common in today's world is psychological murder. Rumors and disparaging remarks destroy a person's reputation and future. Spend any time in the bowels of an organization and you'll hear the whispered comments and accusations that comprise psychological murder. "This strategy is the dumbest one I've every heard. What have they been smoking to think it's going to work?" is a comment from a senior executive of a large medical products company. "She must be sleeping with someone to get that kind of job" is a comment from a mid-level manager of a federal government agency. And so it goes—a few damaged reputations here, a few put-downs there, and pretty soon no one's left standing. Just another murderous day in corporate-land.

✻ A young manufacturing executive was engaged in a "no-holds-barred" battle with the head of quality control. In an all-out effort to win the war, he invented problems that he accused the quality department of not fixing. Whenever the quality-control people showed up to work on the "problems," he told them, "I fixed them already." He went so far as to call the quality-control department head in the middle of the night to report an "emergency," only to have the "emergency" fixed by the time the sleepy department head arrived on the scene.

After two months, the department head resigned. Years later, the manufacturing executive learned that the man had committed suicide a year after his resignation, depressed over being unable to find work.

The executive wept the night he learned about the tragedy, and many nights thereafter.

This kind of "murder" is precisely the behavior that the 6th Commandment of Success cautions you against. You can't achieve a successful career built on the bodies of those you've eliminated. You cannot climb a ladder of success in life constructed from the bones of those you've used and discarded.

The 6th Commandment of Success urges you to take the initiative to positively impact others' lives, help them learn and grow, present them with stimulating opportunities, and be a safety net for their failures. It is related to the 4th Commandment, but whereas the 4th Commandment focuses on learning and growing yourself, the 6th Commandment focuses on coaching and developing others.

Coach Others to Grow Their Souls and Develop a More Fulfilling Life

A coach is "a vehicle to transport people." As a coach, your challenge is to transport people to higher and higher levels of personal and professional fulfillment. As a coach, you help people develop career capabilities—the skills and knowledge necessary to succeed in the world of business. In addition, you also help people develop life skills, such as learning, putting others first, gracing and honoring others with their words, and all the rest of the Ten Commandments of Success. You help ordinary people do extraordinary things. It's an important responsibility.

✿ Ferid Murad was the first member of his family to graduate from high school. On his path to earning an M.D., he got lots of coaching and mentoring from individuals, including customers in his family's restaurant. As part of his desire to pay back all the help he'd received from others, he sponsors promising students from less-affluent families. One student particularly stands out: a twenty-six-year-old who reported to work in his lab in full biker dress. Nine years later, this student moved with Murad to Stanford University and then went on to head his own medical school department. Nothing has distracted Murad from his task of mentoring/coaching young people, not even receiving the 1998 Nobel Prize in medicine. Murad has said, "Trainees are like offspring, your children. It makes me feel very good when they've done well and when they go on and help others. It's like building a pyramid."

✿ Jerre Stead, chairman of Ingram Micro, talks about coaching Larry, an Ingram vice president. Stead joined Larry to visit several potential customers in Larry's new territory. On their way to the hotel that night Larry said, "It's really exciting to watch you work the crowd, asking questions and developing personal relationships. I learned a lot watching you. Now I'm itching to get in and do it myself. Put me in, coach. Let me lead the sessions tomorrow."

Stead couldn't have been more pleased. It was just what he wanted to have happen: The person he was coaching was thirsting to get in the game and try his skills. The next morning Larry asked the questions. Stead reinforced Larry's victories while helping him see how he might improve. Larry made copious notes and, like fine wine, got better as time went on. "It's exciting to watch Larry master this skill," Stead told me. "Just last week he left me a long voice mail telling us how successful this question-asking process was with a prospective customer in Hong Kong."

Great Coaches Teach Life Lessons

My reverend is an extraordinary coach. One day, I watched him teach a sullen and withdrawn teenager a great life lesson. On the verge of self-alienation, Billy slouched in the corner, the crotch of his frayed, oversized jeans and his big-link key chain dragging on the floor. In front of the congregation, the pastor enlisted Billy's reluctant help in an activity that appealed to Billy's strength: an arm-wrestling match between Billy and the reverend.

The two assumed their clasped-hands positions across the table, staring at each other. Billy easily won the first round, as the reverend didn't offer any resistance. Billy looked surprised. "Guess you won that one," the reverend said, moving their hands to the initial clasped-hands position. "Billy, I forgot to tell you that your dad promised a dime a win," the reverend said. In the second round, he offered some initial resistance, but went limp again after a few seconds. Billy won the second round. "Guess that's two dimes for you," he said, moving their hands to the original upright position. This time the reverend offered strong resistance. Billy struggled for an instant, then a smile crossed his face and his hand went limp.

"That's right, Billy," the reverend said smiling. "Now you've caught on. Let's both get lots of dimes. He called out to Billy's father, "Hey, John. Hope you brought a stash tonight." With that, both Billy and the reverend quickly moved their clasped hands back and forth in perfect unison. The audience broke out in laughter and applauded.

"Billy," the reverend asked, "what's the lesson here?"

"Cooperating wins me more dimes. Dad, you owe me two and a half bucks."

Here's an example of a great coach in action. Rather than telling or preaching to Billy, he helped him learn a valuable lesson about respectful inclusion.

Coaching Is a Marriage, Not a One-Night Stand

Coaching isn't an event that happens occasionally. It's a full-time-plus commitment to be there for the person you are coaching—whenever, wherever, however—to help him or her grow.

> ✿ I coach an executive of a manufacturing company. I spoke with him every day during a difficult executive personnel situation. We volleyed e-mails and voice mails between us like a Wimbledon finals match. He'd call me with an observation, and I'd volley back both a compliment and a suggestion. He'd call me with a report, and I'd respond with more compliments and suggestions. I knew that as his coach I had to stay engaged until he no longer needed my support. Within weeks, the calls, e-mails, and voice mails grew less frequent as the executive grew more confident about his ability to resolve the situation. We now talk once a month. He's capable of handling those difficult situations on his own.

Continue to Raise the Bar

First-time skiers don't fly down the slope. It takes a great deal of practice. A good coach knows that you don't promise immediate rides down the big hill after the first lesson (except maybe on your rear end, if you're foolish enough to try). A good coach sets the initial expectations and then raises them (first staying up on the skis, then moving forward on the skis, then . . . well, you get the picture). Incremental steps are the only way to achieve mastery of any skill. A good coach acknowledges current achievements while raising the bar for future performance.

☼ One of my customers owned a small manufacturing firm. In order to help him grow his sales, we organized a series of phone calls with groups of customers to talk about industry developments, technological changes, etc. The owner always assumed that he would be only a small supplier to these much larger customers. During the initial calls, I asked four customers their predictions for the industry over the next several years and how the best supplier could meet their needs. Those questions triggered an hour-long conversation. The owner was elated. "I can't believe it. We've actually got a shot at becoming a big supplier to these folks." Raising the bar helped the owner see that he had a much greater opportunity than he'd ever imagined.

Focus on Progress, Not Perfection

No one's perfect. Not even you or me. And that's okay. Your job as a coach is to provide a continuous stream of affirming reinforcement about current performance levels and continually encourage the person you are coaching to keep learning.

☼ Follow the Weight Watchers approach. Weight Watchers is not about making people feel *bad* about not losing weight. It's about helping people feel *good* about losing weight. Like Weight Watchers, "weigh in" everybody at the beginning of the meeting and praise the heck out of those who have achieved their goals. Help those who didn't realize their expectations figure out what they can do to be more successful next time.

Focus folks on the thrill of what your "coachees" are becoming—whether it's being thin or schussing down that slope—not the pain of what they have not yet become.

APPLICATION

Pick one person you coach. How can you help that person . . .

• be more fulfilled than they are today?

_____

_____

_____

_____

_____

_____

_____

_____

• see beyond what they are today to what they might become tomorrow?

_____

_____

_____

_____

_____

_____

_____

_____

_____

_____

_____

_____

Build Stages for Great Performances

Help People See the Bigger Picture

Do you suffer from tunnel vision? I do. It's easy to get caught up in what you're doing and ignore everything else that's going on.

✿ One of my relatives decided to move to another city to find work. He ran irrigation pipe for a living and felt that the opportunities would be better there. He packed up his household goods, loaded his wife and kids into the car, and took off. He e-mailed me a few weeks later looking for some coaching. It seems that he was having difficulty finding a pipe-laying job. I suggested that he look in some other related fields, such as plumbing and general maintenance. These ideas, along with his hustling, brought to the surface several interim opportunities. He got a maintenance supervisor's job in a plant that turned out to the best job he'd ever had. He'd been stuck in identifying himself as an irrigation pipe layer and didn't see the opportunities in the next field.

Create Opportunities for People to Practice Their Voice Lessons

Coaches do much more than ask questions or make suggestions. Coaching is an active, engaging role. You're in the people-growing business. The folks you coach need venues to sing the songs in their hearts. Go find them a theater that provides a stage upon which they can practice their skills and talents.

✻ Itka, a former student of mine, was an extraordinar-
ily skilled C++ programmer. He wanted to develop a
project management skill in order to learn how to
better understand the needs of large-scale systems
integration. I contacted a few firms I knew and
found two internship opportunities for him. He
spent seven months with a company in the heavy
construction industry, learning its project-
management process. He went on to head a major
project-management business and today has his own
consulting firm. I helped find the theater for Itka in
which he could learn how to perform on the big
stage. He seized the opportunity and made the most
of it.

✻ Dick was the head of a major company in San Diego.
He was also the chairman of the United Way. One
day over lunch he told me, "I never learned more
than when I led the United Way. We had lots of chal-
lenges—it was just after the big scandal in New York,
and the PR was just awful. I learned what it takes to
motivate senior folks to volunteer their time: clear
goals, lots of positive feedback on their contributions, and effective administrative systems that
deliver the materials they need to do their jobs. I
took those same lessons into my company and dramatically moved the needle." Volunteer work has its
own rewards. It's a great teacher.

The world is awash in opportunities for those you are
coaching to practice and develop their abilities to sing. Find
the venue for them.

✿

Visit the Best to Raise Sights and Expectations

Many folks worry that other people are doing things better than they themselves do them. I *know* that other people are doing things I do better than me. So I go out and regularly study those folks and learn from them. It's hard to do on an emotional level, as each of us wants to think of ourselves as the best. And it's time consuming to visit others. It's much easier to hide behind the "I'm-too-busy" shield or put off a visit with "call me next week."

Seeing Excellence in Action Helps People Visualize a Way to Do It Themselves

Try describing lobster to someone who's never tasted it. Hard, isn't it? The same is true about describing excellent customer service to someone who's never seen or experienced it. Encourage the people you coach to experience lobster and excellent customer service so they can visualize themselves eating it or doing it.

✿ Find companies that are doing something particularly well and encourage the person you're coaching to visit them in order to learn from them.

✿ Identify some particularly gifted person in an area in which the person you are coaching is interested and encourage him or her to spend time with that person.

Capitalize on the Learning

Translate the learning into specific, concrete actions. Look over the wall to see how others do things. It's a wonderful way to expand horizons, gain new insights, and raise the level of expectations. Be ready with some ideas for specific applications when the person you are coaching comes back and says,

"I didn't realize X was possible. Now I realize that X and Y and Z are also possible—and I want to figure out a way that I can do those."

> # Create the theater, the stage, and the rehearsal sites for your coachee's great performance.

Be the Emotional Bridge to the Future: Give Affirming Support

Be There for the Person You Are Coaching: Be an Ear, a Smile, an Encouraging Word, and Some Sage Advice

It's very difficult to make the trip to tomorrow when it requires giving up the comforts of today. You know what's expected today—both you and everyone else. Okay, today may not be everything you *really want*, but it's easier to complain about it than take steps toward the future. After all, the future is totally uncertain. You can't know what's really going to happen. As Kris Kristofferson sang, "We love the comfort of our chains."

That's why you, as the coach, are so important. It's scary stepping off into the great unknown. While you can't take the risk for the person you are coaching, you can be his or her emotional bridge to tomorrow. You can be there—as many people have been there for you in the past—to talk, share, commiserate, and celebrate. Your presence provides the guardrail.

> ✿ I struggled for a long time to help my firm break into the textile dye market. Nothing seemed to work. One day over lunch with my "mastermind" group, an attorney suggested, "Have you thought about interviewing a few of the folks who rejected your offers? Maybe they could tell you what you're doing wrong." His coaching hit me like a two-ton truck. Of course, talk to the noncustomers. I was too fixated on my efforts. My mental blinders completely prevented me from getting what I wanted. After two conversations with noncustomers, I had a clear picture of what we needed to do. The answer was simplicity itself: Because this was a custom design market, we had to

listen carefully to the customer's needs and tone
down the hard-sell approach I was using. The attorney acting as my coach called me several times during
this difficult time. He encouraged me to keep looking for better answers and helped me handle the
negative responses I was getting. His faithful presence
made all the difference to me.

Focus on the Thrill of Who the Person You Coach Is Becoming

I've heard the following from the podium several times:
"Eagles don't have rearview mirrors." I'm also told, "Mountain climbers always look up, focusing on the next hill to
climb." Unfortunately, I'm a slow learner. I hear these very
plausible messages and continue to beat myself up about the
poor comparisons I make against some arbitrary standard.
Yes, I've only gotten two chapters written thus far, and I said
I'd have five by this time. But they're great chapters and I
have a handle on what the balance of the book will be. I tend
to criticize myself for doing anything less than completing
the book. My coach helps me see that I've made great progress
toward my ultimate goal of having a successful book.

Not to play a word game, but this is an attitude issue. Is
the glass half-empty or half-full? Is it partly cloudy or partly
sunny? It's very tough making the journey. It's easier to ease
up and slip back into the old ways. As a coach, emphasize the
progress your coachee is making and focus on the future steps
that he or she will take to keep moving forward. The vital
questions for you to pose are: "Are you making progress
toward achieving what you said you wanted to be?" and "How
can you move the process faster?" Neither you nor your
coachee can change the past. Be determined to make the
future different by focusing on what your coachee is becoming, not what he or she isn't. Be your coachee's emotional
bridge to the future.

You Shall Not Commit Adultery

Keep Your Commitments

"I was just too tired to move, your honor," Rosa Parks said softly.

The judge ruled that the African–American woman didn't have to give up her seat to a white person and move to the back of the bus.

The governor of Alabama called the judge *"an integrating, carpet-bagging, scallywagging, race-mixing, bald-faced liar."* Another national organization called him *"the most hated man in Alabama"* and burned a cross on his lawn.

His colleagues on the bench shunned him. He required a police escort for years.

But none of that deterred Frank Minis Johnson Jr. from approving Martin Luther King's march in Selma, Alabama, as *"an exercise of their right to demonstrate peacefully against the enormity of the wrongs they were suffering."* When offered the opportunity to lead the FBI, Johnson decided that being a federal judge in Alabama was more important.

By his actions, Johnson demonstrated all three dimensions of the commitment envisioned in the 7th Commandment of Success: commitment to actions that reflect one's own values, commitment to helping others' live according to their values, and commitment to the achievement of the group's higher purpose or vision.

Be Prepared to Make the Big "C"

Frank Johnson believed in the Constitution. His personal commitment to uphold its values led him to make a string of rulings concerning the civil rights of African Americans.

And what is the price of these commitments? Isn't everything for sale, given the right price? No, your commitments are not for sale—at any price. Patrick Henry summarized this in his famous words, "Give me liberty or give me death."

Commitment Is the Foundation of All Relationships

Keeping one's word—one's commitment—is the foundation of all human relationships. Keeping commitments—to a spouse, a fellow worker, a customer, or a community member—is the basis for all productive relationships. It's also a basic prerequisite for becoming the captain of your fate and the master of your soul.

Choose First, Commit Second, Give Up Options Third—That's What Makes It Hard to Do

Many people struggle with the big C word because it involves giving up options. When you commit to A, you give up B, C, etc. In the relationship world, committing to marry Sam means giving up Jim, John, and Brad. That's hard to do sometimes and is sometimes why extramarital affairs occur. In the organizational world, many leaders find it hard to turn down requests for worthwhile projects. They really want to have a quality program *and* a work/life enhancement program *and* a day care program. In their effort to do it all, they become equal-opportunity starvers. They say yes to all the worthwhile things that come across their desks. However, because of the reality of limited resources, this actually means they are saying no to all of them.

The complexity of life makes it difficult to commit—and then keep your word about your commitment. There's just so much crying out for your resources. There's the kids' Little League and music lessons and scouting—all valuable activities. Then there are the church activities—bible study, youth group, and men's group. Service and community organizations join the "commit-to-me" chorus. Now add the many business- and profession-related activities that press in on you. And don't forget that commitment to make time for that special someone in your life and the time for yourself to exercise.

To Thine Own Self Be True and Thou Can Be False to No Man

What Are You Prepared to Die For?

What are you prepared to die for?" the imposing-looking speaker thundered from the platform. I squirmed along with the rest of the audience. "Do you know?" he asked in an even louder voice. More squirming. I wasn't sure I had a quick answer to either question. "Don't you think you'd better find out? If you don't stand for something," he said, "then you'll fall for anything." His words haunted me for years. What was I really willing to sacrifice my life for? I gave money to help starving children in Africa. I spent days of my life working with teenage drug addicts. But sacrifice my life? That was an entirely different matter. He was right. Until I got clear on what I really stood for, I would (and did) fall for anything in my search of the next great thing.

Be Prepared to Die for Your Soul's Agenda— Once You Get Clear on What It Is

Getting clear on your true values is easy—once you make the commitment to do it. But there's the rub. It's hard work getting past all the "shoulds" and "musts" you've learned from your parents, teachers, friends, and bosses. That list is very long indeed—all the way from "you should wear clean underwear every day" ("you never know when you'll be in an accident") to "you must show up to work on time." The problem with the "shoulds" and "musts" is that it's hard to know when they're really someone else's agenda, not your own.

Align Your Actions with Your Internal Commitments

For years I struggled to become a more empowering leader. But all my efforts failed. My people kept "forcing" me to make decisions that I thought they should be making. My epiphany occurred during an exit interview with an employee. When I asked him to identify the problem with my empowerment efforts, he said, "Jim, the problem is you don't really believe that anyone else has a better answer than you. So you ask people to make decisions, but you keep second-guessing them and arguing with them when their answer is different than yours. Save us all time and aggravation, just tell us what you want, and we'll do it." I didn't like those words, but I came to see that the employee was absolutely correct. My empowerment efforts didn't improve until I decided that I wanted my new empowerment behavior more than I wanted my old micro-management values.

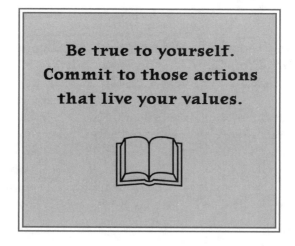

**Be true to yourself.
Commit to those actions
that live your values.**

Help Others to Realize Their Commitments

Align Your Commitments across Your Universe

You are your brother's keeper and your sister's keeper and the keeper for all the members of your family. Help them live richer, fuller, more meaningful lives—first, because it's consistent with your inner commitments to live your own core values, and second, because it enables them to implement their own commitments in order to live their core values.

Align Your Actions with Longer-term Commitments to Helping Others Become the Captains of Their Fates and the Masters of Their Souls

Invest in the longer-term interests and commitments of all those members of your extended family.

Align Long-term Business Interests with Employee's Short-term Salary Interests

It's easy to talk about commitment, particularly for someone else. But it's a different story when it comes to *your own* money. What you are willing to reach into your pockets and peel off dollar bills to support speaks volumes about your real commitment.

> ☼ The fire that destroyed the Malden Mills factory in Methuen, Massachusetts, posed a real problem for both the workers in the plant and the $400 million textile manufacturer. It would take eight months to rebuild the factory—an enormous amount of time to be without product to sell and income to spend on salaries, etc. Acting on his desire to enable his

workers to continue to fulfill their commitments, owner Aaron Feuerstein reached into his pocket and paid workers their full salaries—at a cost of $1.5 million a week. "The community relies upon our payroll. We just had to do it," he said.

Align Personal Aspirations with Organizational Financial Goals

Help people merge their personal commitments with the organization's strategic and financial goals.

> ✿ One organization I know uses the following team-based process: Each person shares his or her personal career goals and aspirations with the team. At the same time, the team defines both its objectives and the individual's performance goals, blending the aspirations of all the individuals on the team with customers' needs and the organization's financial goals. The team works hard to create the circumstances in which doing organizational work also satisfies individual goals and aspirations.

Get Personally Involved in Aligning Commitments

You can't delegate the alignment process. It's *your* body in front of their eyes working the alignment issues. Anything less is DOA—Dead on Arrival.

Show Your Heart's Commitment to Handle a Difficult Situation

Commitment is a personal contact activity. It's easy to send dollars to cure world hunger. After all, it's only money—and you can just cash in a few options if you have to and pay for it. It's very hard to take a week out of your life to help the displaced people of Honduras rebuild their homes devastated by the hurricane. That time is irreplaceable.

☼ William H. Peace ran Westinghouse's Synthetic Fuels division in the early 1980s. One of his mandates was to reduce costs (for "costs," read "jobs"). However, in a small division—130 people—jobs come with faces and mortgages. When the fifteen employees to be dismissed were finally chosen, Bill decided to tell the folks himself. He felt he owed it to them. The meetings were very difficult. Most people took the layoffs very hard. Bill just listened and explained over and over again why it was necessary to sacrifice the few in order to save the many. By the end of their emotion-packed interview, most people shook his hand and thanked him for his time.

Sometimes events play tricks on you. Months later, Bill went looking to rehire those folks. It seems that the division had been sold and the new owner wanted to grow it. All fifteen former employees came back, several leaving high-paying jobs they'd found in the interim. The reason: Bill Peace's personal commitment to them.

☼ Personal involvement also works in the kitchen. It's heck raising teenagers. I would rather visit the dentist, personally. But I've found that spending time together as a family every week helps to align our family's busy schedules and ease the pain of both parenting and growing up. Here's a sample of the results of a recent family meeting. The actual weekly performance is outlined in capital letters:

Teenage Son
School: Turn in all homework on time, pass all subjects (with a minimum grade of B), behave attentively in class, participate, work hard, and keep on-task. GOOD PERFORMANCE. WORK DONE ON TIME. GOOD GRADES THIS WEEK.

Home: Pick up after yourself, leave no trail. REASONABLY GOOD. LEFT KITCHEN TRAIL TWICE DURING THE WEEK. KEPT BOOKS AND CLOTHING OUT OF THE REST OF THE HOUSE.

Church: Attend on Sunday; participate in youth activities. GOOD.

Mother
Drive son to school and all scheduled events. DONE. Arrange for transportation to wedding in July for all kids. THREE OF THE SEVEN COMPLETED. DID NOT RECEIVE INFORMATION FROM THE OTHERS YET. WILL FINISH NEXT WEEK.

Father
Attend weekly family therapy sessions. DONE. Develop landscaping plan with José and get the big tree in front replaced. PLAN COMPLETED AND DISCUSSED WITH JOSÉ. BIG TREE ORDERED, TO ARRIVE AND BE PLANTED NEXT WEEK.

Alignment, through personal involvement, brings a focus and power that helps everyone succeed. Involve yourself to get all the noses lined up and pulling in the same direction and you can do anything.

The alignment process is not easy. People will not always know automatically how to either articulate their commitments or work cooperatively to align them with others'. In fact, most folks will enter your life *not* knowing how to do this, having been well trained *not* to speak their minds, tell the truth, or work together in other phases of their lives. Help them to sort out their soul interests, discuss them, and work together to achieve them.

**Align actions so that
all members of your
extended family
can achieve their
personal commitments.**

Align Actions to Achieve Personal Commitments and the Greater Purpose

Visions of the Greater Purpose Must Be a REAL Greater Purpose

Henry Ford said it well in 1915: "Wealth, like happiness, is never attained when sought after directly. It always comes as a by-product of providing a useful service." There's not much to add to that statement. Many other organizations and individuals similarly focus their long-term commitments on adding social value—and match their actions to them.

> ✿ ServiceMaster, the $2 billion cleaning giant, has as part of its vision the words, "Honoring God in All We Do" and "Grow People." It opens and closes every meeting with a prayer and offers one of the richest ranges of educational programs available in any company.

> ✿ AES, a publicly traded energy company, makes its decisions at the lowest possible level in the organization, basing them primarily on the company's values: integrity, fairness, fun, and social responsibility. AES practices "open-book management," in which every employee has complete access to all financial records (all AES employees are treated as insiders by the SEC as a result). Rather than hire professionals to handle most of the typical home-office activities, such as auditing, human resource management, and purchasing, AES's line employees perform these tasks, thus giving everyone an opportunity to learn and grow.

Align Actions to Achieve the Greater Purpose

Jerre Stead is one of those unusual persons for whom empowerment is a natural state. He didn't have to learn it; he's always done it. But he recognizes that it's not natural for most other people. So one of his long-term personal commitments is to teach people how to empower themselves and others. It's a crusade for Stead. He's developed the Three P's to help him empower people: the *power* to search out the facts, the *protection* to surface the issues, and the *permission* to tell anybody the truth.

> ✿ An engineer in the Lexington, Kentucky, facility at Square D came up with an idea to change the electrical box from metal to plastic. He believed this would lower costs. As you can imagine, his challenge to the status quo produced quite an impassioned debate. He sought coaching from Jerre Stead.
>
> Stead gave the engineer the *power* to investigate the possibility. He provided him the *protection* he needed by arranging for time away from his regular job and a small budget to finance his research. Stead also gave him *permission* to present his findings to an open-minded audience, including himself. It turned out that the engineer was right. The plastic decorator wall switches in your home today are the result of that innovation.

Stead's Three P's enabled the engineer to take actions that fulfilled three separate commitments by three different entities: the engineer's personal commitments to find new and better products; the organization's commitments to long-term growth; and Stead's commitment to spread the practice and gospel of empowerment.

Today's actions must contribute to the achievement of the greater purpose—or else you're wasting your time and everyone else's as well. Keep your hands on the present and your eyes on the future. Align your actions to achieve both at the same time.

Ensure that today's actions . . .

- fulfill today's commitments—both to yourself and others

- contribute to the group's higher purpose

Be the Sterling Example of the Behavior You Want Others to Adopt

B y now you've probably figured it out: You must be the example of this and every other Commandment of Success. Be the exemplary example of aligning your daily actions with:

✵ your commitment to your personal values

✵ the fulfillment of the personal commitments of others across your universe

✵ achievement of the group's vision

People will watch you and emulate what you do—the good, the bad, and the ugly.

✵ I've had the "privilege" of hearing my own words coming out of my son's mouth. My eldest son is loud and demanding with his children. I suspect that he's subconsciously repeating the parenting style he learned from me. I was a powerful role model for him. I taught him to show his caring for his children with a loud and demanding demeanor. Given the wisdom of hindsight, I wish that I had been smarter sooner. He might be less loud and demanding with his children today, as I have learned to become with age and experience.

✺ Mort Meyerson helped Ross Perot build EDS into a very successful company based upon the basic corporate values of "work, work, and more work." Years later, when he rejoined Perot at Perot Systems, he saw that the old EDS way no longer applied. He changed his behavior to model his new "develop others" ethic. He stopped attending every meeting and making decisions. He made himself much more available through e-mail and voice mail. Meyerson knew he had to demonstrate his commitment to his new values in order to encourage others to adopt his new behavior.

✺ Michael Josephson, founder of the Josephson Institute of Ethics, learned a lesson about modeling behavior while searching for a preschool for one of his children. Both he and his wife want the best for their children but lead very active lives. They discovered a highly rated preschool forty-five minutes away and a less highly rated one just down the street. Michael wanted to send his daughter to the neighborhood school in order to save the hour and a half round-trip drive. His wife challenged him, "Is the hour and a half more important than the best education for your daughter? Either you live your values or you don't believe in them—and if you don't believe in them, why should anyone else?" He's driving!

Do *you* model the values you want others to adopt? If you don't, they won't!

APPLICATION

What one action can you take today to set the example for everyone to see you . . .

living your values and fulfilling your vision?

_____
_____
_____
_____
_____
_____
_____
_____

leaving a legacy to the next generation?

_____
_____
_____
_____
_____
_____
_____
_____
_____
_____
_____
_____
_____
_____

You Shall Not Steal

8th Commandment

Always Deliver Your Best

Tony Kerlavage was a protein chemist who conducted his work deep in the laboratories of the National Institutes of Health in the 1980s. It was not a bad job. In fact, there was a long line of people waiting to get into NIH to do similar work. But it wasn't enough for Tony. He liked working on cutting-edge projects, not the run-of-the-mill work he was doing. He needed more of a challenge to fill the hunger in his soul. He stumbled upon cloning and became fascinated with the process. He really loved the computerized cloning sequencers. So he launched his own personally designed Ph.D.-type program. He studied textbooks, read everything he could get his hands on, signed up for specific classes, and cornered knowledgeable people, learning all he could from them. He set out to master entirely new skills in molecular-biological and database management, which he combined with his protein chemical background.

Last time I heard, Tony was directing a seventeen-person bioinfomatics department at the Institute for Genomic Research. He and his staff were using a bank of computerized DNA sequencers and generating medical breakthroughs. Craig Venter, president of the institute, said, "Tony's background is . . . [in] the hottest demand in the field."

Tony's journey from an NIH researcher to a cutting-edge technology leader in less than ten years is a great example of the 8th Commandment of Success: Always do your best.

Beware the Victimitis Plague:
It Robs You of Your Birthright

Tony is one of many ordinary people—like you and me—who practice the essence of the 8th Commandment of Success and perform extraordinary feats as a result. He demonstrates that making and passionately following the commitment to always deliver your best helps you become the master of your fate and the captain of your soul.

In today's world, where opportunity abounds, there are many folks who remain unmotivated to grow their souls or to do their best. The fruit is heavy in the field. Get yourself a ladder and go pick some. Why is there so much disaffection? What's gone wrong? By not delivering the best you have to offer, you steal from yourself and all those who both depend on you and upon whom you depend. You become the ultimate victim.

The Victim's Lament: "They Did It to Me"

Victimitis runs rampant throughout the land. It resides in hearts and heads across the country. Its principle manifestation is blaming the other guy, the situation, the system, the environmentalists, the president, the liberals, the conservatives, or the company. Don't sing the victimitis song. Get ready to belt out your best—always.

Who Did It to Whom?

Examine two different pictures. Picture one occurs at 2:19 P.M. in an office in the executive suite of a large company. Finova stands at her desk, chatting with two other secretaries. Her boss is in a meeting. She's been there for about an hour while the phone rings and rings and the "you've got mail" announcement chimes incessantly on the computer monitor.

Unopened mail is piled on her desk. "I'll get to it before he comes out of his three o'clock meeting," she tells one of her coworkers, "and if I don't, I don't. He'll never know the difference." Finova's attitude is a picture of poor motivation and low commitment level if ever I saw one.

Picture two occurs ten hours later. It is after midnight. Finova is at home, bent over a sewing machine in a neat, carefully arranged home/office setting. She's about halfway done with a very colorful quilt. She's been working without a break now for almost three hours. Her husband opens the door and says, "It's getting late, darling, when are you coming to bed?" "About forty minutes or so," Finova replies. "I need to get all this hemming finished so Kathy can come in tomorrow and lay the pattern. That way I can make some pretty good progress on it over the weekend." Finova's dedication is a great example of high commitment to deliver the best.

But the unmotivated Finova in the office and the deeply committed Finova at home is the same person. What's the difference? We asked Finova. She answered: "My boss is terrible. He's so unappreciative of anything I do that I've stopped doing anything but the barest of basics for him. And you know what? He hasn't noticed anything yet." This is victimitis in full bloom.

The real message is: You make the choice every time. It's your call whether you'll do your best, as Finova does when working on her quilt, or withhold your best efforts, as she does when she's at the office. The boss is irrelevant. The company is irrelevant. Your family/place of birth/skin color is irrelevant. In life, the ball is always in your court and the shot is always your call.

Victims Steal from Themselves

Thieves steal things from others, usually money, art, and property. Victims steal from themselves by not delivering the best they have to offer. Shakespeare wrote, "Who steals my purse steals trash. . . . But he that filches from me my good name / Robs me of that which not enriches him / And makes me poor indeed." Victims sully and depreciate the value of their good names by delivering less than their best. When you deliver less than your best, you deliver damaged, inferior goods—with your name on them. Every action you take influences your name, good or otherwise, just as every turn at bat influences a baseball player's batting average.

There's no substitute for the attitude expressed by major league baseball player Tony Gwynn, who joined the very exclusive club of three-thousand-hit players in 1999 and who said, "Every time I come to bat I'm reminded about how fortunate I am to be here. I owe it to every one of those fans to do my best every time." Tony does his best for his fans, yes, but he does his best because doing his best is what fulfills Tony's soul.

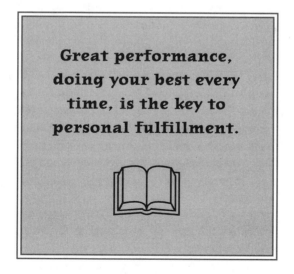

Great performance, doing your best every time, is the key to personal fulfillment.

Focus on Helping Others Fulfill Their Destinies: It Also Helps You Fulfill Yours

People Suffer from Lack of Focus, Not Lack of Motivation

My experience tells me that while victimitis is an epidemic, it need not be fatal. People don't lack motivation. In fact, I've seen folks take safety guards off machines so they can accomplish their work faster—even though they're risking their fingers, or worse. What people *do* lack is the focus on what to do. Most folks work hard, but on the wrong tasks. That frustrates them and may be what leads to bouts of victimitis.

> ✵ In the 1960s and 1970s, IBM sold a high-priced product—but customers really didn't care. IBM bragged it sold "a good night's sleep." And that it did. Along with many others, I've got my own IBM story: In response to a computer crash at our company, IBM folks showed up over the weekend to get us up and running. I didn't care about the cost of the machine or the nature of the software. They were there for me—that's all I knew and cared about. In those days IBM had great focus: customer service. IBM delivered its considerable talents and built the greatest company of its time.

Get the Real Experts Involved in Defining Great Performance

It took me a long time to realize that the real judges of performance who can answer the question "What is great performance?" are the people to whom you're delivering the great performance. If you're a secretary, you need to find out what your boss thinks great performance from you is. If you're a mom, your children need to tell you what your great performance is for them.

✿ I worked with the head of a Heating, Ventilating and Air Conditioning (HVAC) company. When I asked him how his customers defined great performance for his firm, he had quick, pat answers: more precise controllers, lower prices, and just-in-time installations. His answers sounded reasonable. "Let's check," I suggested. He agreed, though he really didn't see the need for the drill. "I know their answers already," he said. He was startled by the information that came back. It seems his customers wanted better teamwork on the work site, lower total costs of ownership (including maintenance), and more design help. He was equally surprised when he asked his managers how they defined great performance from him personally. They wanted fewer decisions from him and more information, not the better financial controls he thought they wanted.

✿ Sam worked in the administration office of a large university. His daughter, an accomplished ballet dancer, won a trip to Russia to perform with several major ballet companies. The trip overlapped the budget submission date for the university. There were always last-minute changes to be made to the budget, and Sam invariably worked 24-7 (around the clock) during that last "crunch" week to get them all done. Sam called in a panic. "I can't disappoint my daughter Sheila and I can't be gone during this time. What am I to do?" I suggested he ask his Bigger Bosses—his wife and daughter—for their advice and suggestions and then ask the same question of his other Big Bosses, his teammates.

They worked it out. Sam went to Russia, taking with him boxes of documents and an arrangement with the university in Moscow to use its computing lab to crunch any numbers he'd need. Sam didn't see much of Moscow on that trip, but he did see every one of Sheila's performances and rehearsals. He was in the audience when she won the Best of Age medal, and he got the amended budget delivered on time to his home university.

Sam delivered great performance for his bosses—his family, his teammates, and his employer—first by asking in advance what *they* defined as great performance for him and then by delivering it. Sam also told me, "It was a most satisfying time for me. I was so proud to see Sheila do so well. I've not been as good a dad to her as I'd like to have been, and this trip opened up new vistas for our relationship. And I learned some ways that I could be a lot more efficient and effective back at work. I feel much better about myself—and that's the best outcome of all."

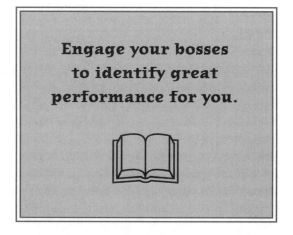

Engage your bosses to identify great performance for you.

Measure, Measure, Measure Great Performance: Use Others' Glasses

How Are We Doing? Everyone Wants to Know

Don't you love to keep score? I know I do. When I'm driving, I count the miles until the next destination. I check my stocks every day to see how much money I made—or lost. I constantly search for numbers that tell me how I'm progressing toward my goals. Today, everyone can know everything. But you can drown in this sea of information. Out of all that you *can* know, what's most important *to* know?

Measure That Which Is Most Important to Your Bosses

See the world through the eyes of your many bosses. Measure how well you're doing in delivering their definition of great performance from you.

> ✿ My grandson Eric applied to college and looked for a soccer scholarship. His dad and I did the background research to identify good business schools with good soccer programs. After reviewing the list with Eric and narrowing it down to seven schools, all three of us scoured the Net to locate as much information as possible about these colleges. We shared this information, exchanging e-mails and discussing it during one of our family get-togethers. Eric chose (with some coaching from his dad, no doubt) three schools he and his dad would visit. Then his dad and I went to work. We contacted people we knew at those

✿

schools to identify the key pieces of information the schools were looking for in an applicant and the preferred way to present that information. I then coached Eric in interviewing techniques. We all scored well on our great performance scoreboard: Eric won a full-tuition soccer scholarship to the university of his choice. Every step of the way we established measures of our great performance—from identifying at least ten schools with both good undergraduate business programs and good soccer programs to securing at least two scholarship offers from the top schools on Eric's list.

Measure against the Best—Anywhere

Whom you choose to measure yourself against will determine how great your great performance is. If you're a player for the New York Yankees baseball team, against whom do you measure yourself, the Little League baseball team down the street or the Cleveland Indians? Obviously, the Yankees compare themselves to the Indians. Why? Because the Indians are consistently one of the strongest competitors in their league.

✿ One of my dearest friends leads a distribution company in a very competitive market. The company averages less than 1 percent return on sales, so any bump, even a relatively minor one, can be disastrous. Early on in our relationship, my friend and I discussed margins. Because it was a tough year, his company's margins had fallen to .5 percent of sales, which was below industry average. His company's best locations that year made 2.26 and 2.08 percent, with several locations in the 1.75–2.0 range. Initially, my friend planned to set the target for .7 percent, but after our conversation he realized that he could do much better than that. As our relationship matured, we had many more discussions about setting the target high enough. Now he sets the target not in terms of percent of sales return, but in terms of being in the third-quartile of margin performance in the industry. While industry margins have deteriorated (I told you this was a tough industry), his company's margins have continued to improve. Measuring against the best, and expecting great performance, makes a difference in financial life.

It's easy in sports or business to identify the best performance level. You can count home runs, touchdowns, and profit dollars. But what's the established standard for the best husband, or the best friend, or the best at virtually any job? Now, this may sound squishy, but I've found that the experts in these kind of "who's-the-best?" questions are the recipients of the service. So wives are the best judges of great husband performance as children are the best judges of great father performance. Similarly, friends are the best judge of ...you get my drift. It all goes back to what we talked about earlier: Sit down and discuss deliverables and measures of your great performance with your bosses.

Everyone Wants Bragging Rights

Everyone I know wants to be the best—at something. Maybe it's having the best garden. Our neighbor Everett keeps us supplied with fresh, homegrown, organic vegetables. He (and we) glory in his reputation as a farmer (not bad for a probation department executive, right?).

Or maybe it's having the best child athlete. One of my sons is a sports nut with his young son. He's enrolled his son in year-round sports. Most of the year, my grandson ends up playing two sports simultaneously. My son feels that the athletic accomplishments of his son are his bragging rights.

✿

Encourage people to seek out the ways they can be best—ways they can deliver great performance—and be recognized for it. Red Auerbach, former coach and president of the Boston Celtics basketball team, said once, "It's not the money that motivates these men to such heights of performance. It's the ring. It's the bragging rights at the old schoolyard."

> ## Always deliver your best to your many bosses— as defined by them. Do it to enable them to live their dreams while enabling you to fulfill yours.
>
>

APPLICATION

Talk to one of your bosses and define . . .
• great performances for you in the coming time period

_____
_____
_____
_____
_____
_____
_____

• how that great performance for you will contribute to your
dreams and those of your boss

_____
_____
_____
_____
_____
_____

• what measure you and your boss will use to know when your
performance is truly great

_____
_____
_____
_____
_____
_____

You Shall Not Give False Testimony
against Your Neighbor

9TH COMMANDMENT

Be an Open Book

Freddie was a final assembler in a manufacturing plant I ran during the 1960s. He was a "sharp looker," and we relied upon his keen eyes to catch defects. However, Freddie was also an alcoholic.

Freddie's drinking was an open secret. One morning, he came in clearly unfit for work. Several of his teammates intercepted him and kept him upstairs in the locker room until he sobered up. When he showed up at the assembly room around noon, I called an emergency meeting and confronted the issue of Freddie's drinking head-on. I asked the assembly team: "What are we going to do? Can we always trust someone to notice Freddie's condition? Are we willing to put our jobs on the line? Are we helping Freddie, or are we just helping him kill himself?"

We formed a "Save Freddie" committee. Every person in the room agreed to do something to help Freddie kick the habit. But nothing could happen until Freddie admitted to being an alcoholic and stated his desire to do whatever it took to stop drinking. The silence must have lasted an eternity. Finally, Freddie stood up and said the magic words.

The story has a happy ending. Freddie got sober and stayed that way. Last I heard, he was a general foreman in a large company and was doing well. He learned what the 9th Commandment of Success is all about: letting your private words and actions reflect who you really are.

The *60 Minutes* Rule: Who Is That Masked Man, Anyway?

F reddie's story might have had a different ending had we had a different climate in the factory. The entire meeting might never have happened. We might have ended up in some court, or in front of some arbitrator, arguing fine points of law and evidence. I'm glad Freddie's case didn't take that path. We might have lost him, and who knows what other awful consequences we might have had to bear?

I encouraged openness in the factory. I shared all the production and quality data with the staff and involved them in all technical, management, and operations decisions. The staff and I had a good relationship that enabled us to talk about Freddie's problem more in a family-like context than in an antagonistic, boss/employee-type way. Such settings discourage the giving of false testimony.

Your Private Words and Actions Are Your True Testimony of Who and What You Really Are

Your words and actions are the messengers from your soul. They reveal the truth about you, what you stand for, and what you really believe. The 9th Commandment of Success parallels the 3rd Commandment, Grace and Honor Others with Your Words. Beyond the 3rd Commandment, though, your private words and actions—which today are more visible— likely reflect your true feelings and are therefore more honest representations of the person who lives within. Given today's increased visibility, it is much easier for others to get beyond your carefully scripted public words to see your truer self.

Is Your Private Testimony Consistent with Your Public Words?

How do you feel about someone who publicly supports equal opportunity yet employs African-Americans as gardeners, housekeepers, etc., sends their children to a private, mostly white school, and socializes with virtually all white people? Do their private words and actions lead you to mistrust their public pronouncements?

How many people do you know who support environmentalism with their checkbooks but do not recycle plastic and paper in either their homes or businesses?

Your Public Treatment of Others Is Your Most Powerful Statement of Your Private Testimony

When asked to identify the most important rule of life, Buddha replied: "reciprocity." To some people this sounds like the biblical Golden Rule: "Treat people the way you want to be treated." I don't think that's what Buddha really meant. Rather, both Buddha and the Ten Commandments teach us to treat people in a way that witnesses and reflects our true feelings and values. That's true inner reciprocity.

✿ Thomas Watson Sr., founder of IBM, bought his newspaper from the same newsstand operator every day. The man often insulted Mr. Watson, along with everyone else. An aide asked Watson why he continued to buy his newspaper from the man, and why he wouldn't insult the newspaper vendor back. Watson gave him a classic 9th Commandment response: "I treat him like a gentleman not because he is a gentleman, but because I am a gentleman." Watson's public actions bore witness to his private testimony.

✿ Imelda lost her husband of many years to cancer. She drew the curtains on her life—as she did over the windows of her home—and grieved for more than a year. "Enough," she told me. "I am not about grief, I am about life. José was about life. I dishonor his memory and insult myself by hiding out. It's time to breathe again and be who I am." Last I heard, she was president of her church. Imelda made her private testimony consistent with her public actions.

All too often, we respond out of anger or hurt, rather than out of the caring and support that reflects our private testimony. Each time we allow our emotions to bear false witness—causing a gap between our private testimony and our public words or deeds—we weaken the bond among our "families" and make it more difficult to help each other become captains of our fates and masters of our souls.

Are Public Words Just a Cover for a Different Private Testimony?

Many times individuals believe that they cannot give honest testimony, so they invent cover-up strategies and give false testimony.

✡ I worked with the leader of a small, high-tech packaging company. He was concerned about the slow pace of innovation in his company. I met with his senior management team, all of whom seemed supportive of doing things differently. Then the questions started to come: Has my process ever worked in a small company of under one hundred persons (they had ninety-one employees on the payroll)? Had my process ever worked in the packaging industry? Had it ever worked in a high-tech company? And so on and so on. Finally I caught on: They were looking for proof that the process had worked in precisely the same circumstances as their company—a statistical impossibility. In truth, they really didn't want to go through the process and were looking to gather enough facts to say to their boss, "It's too risky because it's never worked in a situation like ours." They couldn't say that to the leader's face directly, so they used a "question-'til-they-drop" cover-up strategy.

✪ I once worked with a door manufacturing company. One of the senior leaders was forever providing extensive statistical details and facts. He'd go on and on about the technical specifications of various products, their applications, their costs, lists of customers, and their individual peculiarities. More than half the time of any meeting was taken up by these "important facts"—even though no one had requested the data. I couldn't find any connection between his facts and the issues under consideration. Finally I gave up. His false testimony—his "global dump"— wore me out, and for the first and only time I returned his boss's retainer fee. "I can't help you. Here's your money back," I told him, and I was glad to get out with my sanity.

You Know It's Going to Be a Bad Day When ...

I've heard the bittersweet joke in executive suites, "You know it's going to be a bad day when you see Mike Wallace and the *60 Minutes* crew in your waiting room." Having Mike Wallace thrust a microphone in your face and ask his pointed questions was, and still is, one of many executives' worst nightmares. Why? *60 Minutes* researchers often manage to expose the gap between public pronouncements and private words and behavior. More than any other TV news show, it has exposed many false testimonies that were offered as fact.

✪ Taval is a very successful consultant. He lives the "good life": frequent international travel at expensive resorts, several homes in fashionable areas, fast sports cars for him, and luxurious sedans for the family. On the surface, he has everything. Yet, he'd die if *60 Minutes* showed up at his door. His eldest son ran away and hasn't been heard from for several years. His eldest daughter is back home with her two fatherless children and no visible means of support. His wife, Elana, is now in her fifth round at the Betty Ford alcoholism clinic. And Taval has the reputation of a "sailor"—having a girl in every port. Taval preaches the need for strategic planning, involving all the stakeholders in a situation. He just doesn't practice it very much himself. Maybe he should listen to his own lectures. His private testimony is quite different from his public words.

Welcome a Visit from *60 Minutes*

Be ready for the members of the *60 Minutes* crew when they show up. In fact, invite them to visit. Live your life so that you'd be proud to tell them anything, show them anything, and take them anywhere. Be certain that your public and private words and deeds are true testimony of who and what you really are. Then you can invite millions of television viewers to critically examine your life and how you've lived it.

> **Make certain that your private testimony reflects who you really are.**

You Live in a Glass House: Get over It and Enjoy the View

Assume that everything you say or do is being recorded and can be available to any interested party. It wasn't that way only a few years ago. People could speak freely in an office behind closed doors or on a telephone without fear that some private word or phrase would be taken (in or out of context) and splashed across the six o'clock news. You could speculate or discuss alternatives among friends or colleagues without fear that years later your speculations or explorations would be evidence in multibillion-dollar lawsuits.

> ✿ Even when you're away from home, don't think the home folks (and the rest of the world as well) can't see what you're doing. Just ask Hansie Cronje, the clean-cut, straight-arrow South African cricket star. He was the cream of the crop in that cleanest of sports, cricket. Yet, he admitted to taking between $10,000 and $15,000 from bookmakers while engaging in "dishonest and prohibited activities" during his tour through India. Through a spokesperson, Cronje said, "For the sake of my Christian convictions, I have decided to reveal my involvement in this matter," after being charged with "cheating, fraud, and criminal conspiracy related to match-fixing and betting." Regardless of his innocence or guilt, the damage is done to Cronje and the sport he loved so dearly.

We live in the age of transparency. To paraphrase the *Miranda* rights warning: "Anything you do or say can and will be held against you in the court of public opinion." Get over wringing your hands about it—it's here. The unforgiving, blinking red light is everywhere, ready to record and report when your private testimony does not match your public words. Let's get on with leveraging this heightened visibility to enhance your truthful testimony, making certain that your words and deeds reflect your true being.

Get In Touch with the Heart and Soul of Your Big Bosses, Bigger Bosses, and Even Bigger Bosses

Get in touch with the heart and soul of the people with whom you travel on the road of life. Get past the politically correct niceties and get down to the real stuff about them as human beings. Learn how they live and think. Get them up on your radar screen and watch closely.

Get Direct Information about Your Bosses

If you make a product, get direct feedback from the users of your product. If you lead a group, put the producers of your product in direct contact with the users.

> ✵ One of the few smart things I did when I became involved with a specialty chemical company was to get those folks who made the products (yes, the technicians on the production line) to talk directly to the customers. They discovered all kinds of new applications and fixed many of the quality problems we were having.

> ✵ Tom Warner, president of Utility Service Express, set up his $30-million-plus plumbing and HVAC business as a collection of semi-independent business units. The local folks were responsible for their own geographic area and customer set. To their local customers, these virtual-entrepreneurs *are* Utility

Service Express. Over the last six years, Warner has grown his business from $19.8 million to $31 million and margins from zero to 15.5 percent.

☼ In my manufacturing plant I shared as much information as I could with everyone in the plant. I got the feeling that many folks really didn't care about the information itself. They squirmed through most discussions. But almost all liked to be included in hearing the information. The value of the sharing was more in my willingness to do it than in the actual content.

Build Systems That Provide Visibility about the Heart Desires of Your Bosses—and Indicate How Well You're Doing in Meeting Those Desires

Capture useful, actionable information and make it accessible to everyone who needs it. It's a challenge, though. You're so awash in information—unorganized bits of it buzzing around like so many flies on a summer's night—it's easy to get distracted by the buzzing flies of disorganized, nonfactual, and difficult-to-understand data. Get focus throughout your universe by organizing all relevant and actionable data and making it readily accessible.

Get the People Who Need the Data to Design How to Get It and Package It

Don't try to be an expert in what *they* need. Get *them* engaged in designing the process—and get out of the way. I let the warehouse people decide how to best measure their progress toward delighting customers. I wasn't close enough to their job to have enough information to make a good judgment.

Get People to Decide the Few Bits of Information That Are Most Valuable to Them

The purchasing people at Ingram Micro decided that fill rates, days of owned inventory, and days of accounts payable were the critical pieces of information they needed in order to maximize their contribution both to their customers' satisfaction and the company's success. So that's exactly what they got.

Make Performance Visible around the Kitchen Table and the Conference Room

Performance data is high on the critical "to know" list. Make certain that everyone knows who's doing what, when it needs to be done, what the outcome will be, and how it will be delivered. This helps people across your universe support and contribute to each other's fulfillment.

> ✿ A neighboring family developed a ritual of sharing weekly "hits, runs, and errors" along with their bagels over Sunday morning breakfast. They call it their "Sunday-morning-going-to-church time." They talk about what each family member is doing, where they need help and support, and what they've accomplished during the week. Their fourteen-year-old daughter told me once, "I know I can count on Alex [her brother] and Mom and Dad to be there for me when I need them, because we've talked about it together. They know I'll help them when they need it. I hate to admit it, but they helped me by getting on my case about this boy I was stuck on a few months ago, distracting me from my soccer and horseback-riding activities. He's gone now—thank goodness—and Misty [her horse] and I are back to being old friends."

Making performance visible across the kitchen table helps everyone live their words.

Avoid Frustrating People and Failing to Meet Your Objectives by Not Having the System in Place

We learned that lesson the hard way at NCR, when pricing decisions were decentralized and given to customer focus teams. Conceptually, the teams were the right ones for making the pricing decision. The problem was that they didn't have accurate cost information upon which to base their decisions or make good ones. The result: frustrated people and revenue-losing pricing—a double whammy.

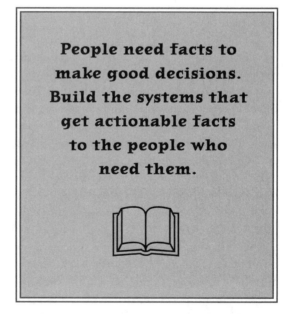

People need facts to make good decisions. Build the systems that get actionable facts to the people who need them.

APPLICATION

With the help of your bosses, what action can you take now to build systems that make intentions, heart desires, and actions visible to all?

_____

_____

_____

_____

_____

_____

_____

_____

_____

_____

_____

_____

_____

_____

_____

_____

_____

_____

_____

_____

_____

_____

_____

_____

_____

_____

Give Honest Testimony: Speak Up, Draw the Lines, and Defend the Values

Get Ready for the "Testimony Moments" That Speak Volumes about Your True Self

Sometimes you just have to stand up for unpopular issues that offend you. These are your "Testimony Moments"—times for you to demonstrate to one and all your true self. Testimony Moments come sometimes while making big decisions: taking a certain job or accepting a "gratuity" for placing an order with a vendor. They sneak up on you while you're just minding your own business, eating ice cream or walking down the street. Pay attention. Testimony Moments sometimes demand that you do something: make a decision, hire a person or not. Other times they allow you to do nothing: You don't speak up when someone is abusing a person of some minority race, you don't stop the robbery going on in the alley you just passed, you don't stop and give first aid to an ailing person on the street. Regardless, remember: That video camera is grinding away, capturing your every move. Whenever Testimony Moments occur, be ready to be the real you.

> ✿ When Hewlett-Packard chose Carly Fiorina to be its chief executive officer, she was only the third woman to pierce the glass ceiling as CEO for a Fortune 500 company. But it took several Testimony Moments by her predecessor, Lew Platt, to set the stage for that to occur. Platt was a typical Hewlett-Packard executive— a white male engineer—who'd never considered gender issues until his wife's death forced him to raise his two preteen girls as a single parent.

That experience convinced Platt that Hewlett-Packard had to do something dramatically different to help its female associates handle the dual roles of parent and professional. While HP managers in general and Platt in particular were "gender-neutral," Platt came to realize that the company's policies weren't flexible enough to help female professionals manage their dual roles. So he sponsored flextime, job sharing, and sabbatical practices. While many organizations have these programs, few actually encourage their employees to use them. Platt pushed his work/life-issues agenda from his CEO perch, writing and speaking about it at every opportunity. In the early 1990s, women employees left the company about twice as frequently as men. Last year the turnover rates were the same—approximately one-third of the industry average.

Platt stepped down as chairman in 1999. When asked what will happen to his work/life issues, he said, "It's up to the company's employees to make sure Hewlett-Packard does not revert to its old self. Specific programs are not important. It's the core values."

✿ Americans have a love-hate relationship with the public schools. Calls for education reform fill the airwaves and newspapers. Everyone has a "proposal." All the white-hot heat, however, has generated precious little real reform. Many people involved in this controversy provide more diatribe than truthful testimony. Jim Sweeney, superintendent of schools for Sacramento, California, decided that the time for jockeying and talk was over. Now was the time for action.

True to his personal values of accountability and serving kids, Sweeney initiated dramatic changes in

California's eighth-largest school district of 52,000 children. He publicly ranks his schools by test scores, holds school administrators and teachers accountable for academic progress, and requires a phonics program in the elementary grades. He took the unpopular stand of promising to replace school administrators and teachers who don't deliver academic progress for their children.

Sweeney has put in place a whole raft of support activities to assist teachers and administrators in achieving their academic progress goals. He celebrates academic achievement, handing out awards for the many schools that moved an average of fifteen points up on the latest test scores.

It's never easy when you're standing up for something in which you truly believe. But then, that's what the 9th Commandment is all about.

Have the Courage to Stand Up for Your Testimony

Do you think of yourself as courageous? You are, you know. If you're at all typical, you've stood up for unpopular things when there was risk involved. You've broken out of your comfort zone more than once to try new ideas and innovative approaches. How do I know? You wouldn't have read this far in this book if you weren't that kind of person.

✡ I worked with a company whose owners developed groundbreaking technology and founded an industry. Their success enabled them to live comfortably for a number of years. While they often loudly proclaimed their commitment to growing the business, they lacked the courage of their words. When other, larger companies knocked-off their products, they chose not to defend their patents, taking a piece of their competitors' business instead. When business got a little tight, they slashed research and development rather than expand their marketing and sales activities to generate more revenue. As their business deteriorated, they continued to slice away at both marketing and selling expenses. Eventually they sold the business on the steps of the bankruptcy court for pennies. Their lack of courage in living their testimony cost them their livelihood.

✿ The Million Mom March against Guns on Mother's Day 2000 attracted people from all walks of life and every part of the country to Washington, D.C. A friend of ours was one of those who traveled there to participate in the march. She didn't go alone; she took her ten-year-old daughter with her. As she explained to a local news reporter, "I wanted my ten-year-old to see hundreds of thousands of people living their beliefs and feel the power of their witnessing their deepest values. It was an invaluable life lesson for her."

✿ David was a juvenile court judge. A lot of troubled teens came through his courtroom—kids as young as thirteen, who'd been doing drugs since they were eight, stealing from stores since they were nine, and hijacking cars since they were eleven. He saw the same ones return to court several times for increasingly severe crimes—and he was frustrated that he couldn't do anything to make a difference. He told me, "Sending them to juvenile hall only deepens their anger and addiction. If we don't help them break the cycle, they'll become hardened criminals and a permanent burden and threat to our society."

David looked around and found several treatment

facilities. He personally visited them all and decided that one offered the best chance for his young offenders. He ordered that treatment program as an alternative to jail for anyone who came before him that he felt had even the slightest chance to make a recovery.

David's actions caused a big stir in his very conservative town. The district attorney publicly criticized him. The supervising judge took him to task for overstepping his boundaries. The mayor suggested that he might have a potential conflict of interest in his relationship with the treatment facility and ordered an investigation.

David was steadfast. He was challenged in the last election and lost to a "law-and-order" candidate. "I'd do it again," he told me. "I don't know how many kids I helped get their lives back on track or saved from a lifetime in jail. Maybe it's only one. I don't know the number—and it doesn't matter. I just know that it was the right thing to do."

Now, there's true courage—standing up for your testimony.

What is this mystical quality called courage? Why is it linked to caring? And what is its relationship to the 9th Commandment? It's simple. Courage is standing up for what you believe in the flag, a principle, or your brother. You believe in helping others become richer, fuller, better human beings. That belief is one of your most central values. Therefore, your belief gives you the courage to pay the price it takes to live the value of helping others grow. It's a circle. Courage comes from the desire and need to help others. In turn, the need to help others feeds your courage. Both courage and helping others grow are evidence of your honest testimony.

Let your courageous
words and actions
be testimony for
who you really are
and what you
stand for.

You Shall Not Covet Your Neighbor's Possessions

Build a Community of People Dedicated to Achieving a Higher Purpose

It was a huge opportunity—and an even larger challenge. A client they'd been chasing for a year called them with an emergency. Their computers kept crashing and they had to have them up and running in twenty-four hours. Could Context Integration do the job?

The task fell to Touray. Though he worked by himself, he was never alone. At 5 A.M. he sent out a 911 distress signal from his laptop describing the problem. The CI knowledge-based system—IAN (Intellectual Assets Network)—contacted individual consultants with expertise in the subject. Within an hour the threaded problem-solving discussion began with colleagues across the country. Prompted by their comments and questions, Touray discovered that one of the URL tag lines was too short, causing the system to shut down. He passed that information on to the client along with the suggested solution. Soon the servers hummed like hummingbirds.

CI's more than two hundred consultants all over the country are connected by the electronic umbilical cord. Unlike most organizations, which are racked with internal jealousies and petty bickering, CI's consultants form a powerful virtual community that is bound together by the common desire to help each other become more competent, more capable, fuller individuals. They have mastered what the 10th Commandment of Success urges: Build a community of people dedicated to achieving their higher purpose.

Feel the Power of a "We" Culture at Work

Getting past the covetous thoughts and preoccupations that divert our individual and collective energies to marshal the power of a common, other-oriented commitment—that's what the 10th Commandment of Success is all about. It's a thing of wonder and awe to experience the power of many minds and hearts, free from the cancerous effects of covetous thoughts, working together as one.

With this last commandment you come full circle—and dig to the deepest level of your being. The purpose: Focus your entire self on helping others become the captains of their fates and the masters of their souls so they—and you— can lead fuller, richer, more meaningful lives. In doing so, you and they achieve a higher purpose.

Thoughts Stain Your Soul and Guide Your Actions

A Greek philosopher said, "The soul is stained by thought." Descartes said, "I think, therefore I am." The 10th Commandment adds, "What you think is what you are. You will carry the stain of your thoughts into eternity. Make certain your thoughts—at their deepest, most private level— support who you really want to be."

Thoughts presage action. You think and then you act: that's the normal pattern. It's hard to think A and do B— particularly if A and B call for widely different actions.

> ✿ I wasted two hours in a meeting last week. I was frustrated watching the participants say A while acting out B: Sarah wants the newly created administrative-assistant position, so she agrees with everything her

boss, Jun, says. Her fawning behavior is unseemly but widespread. Sarah claims to support the new innovative program that's under discussion. But Jun secretly wants to scuttle the program so he can resurrect it later under Sarah's aegis. Sarah constantly broadens the scope of the program, hoping it will crash from overweight.

Pat wants the project coordinator position now occupied by Sam, another participant at the meeting. Pat criticizes everything Sam says. While Pat claims to want to design the best program, her real effort is to discredit Sam so she can get his position.

Just one more typical day in organization-land, where private agendas of coveting create dysfunctional public actions.

Drive Out the Cancer of Coveting with the Antidote of Otherness

Coveting what others have becomes a cancer that consumes you. It's an addiction, like tobacco, alcohol, and cocaine. It takes over your life and controls your every waking moment. The best antidote: Fill your days with other-oriented thoughts and actions. Crowd out the covetous thoughts—give them no place to rest within your being—with preoccupations such as, "How can I best help Sam find fulfillment? How can I best help Sarah live a richer, fuller life? How can I best help Jun find more meaning in his life?"

Focus on helping others find richer, deeper meanings in life to remove the cancer of coveting from your soul.

APPLICATION

What one thing have you coveted recently? (Don't be embarrassed; we've all coveted things others have. Just be honest.)

_____

_____

_____

_____

_____

_____

_____

_____

_____

_____

What one other-oriented action can you take to drive out that coveting cancer?

_____

_____

_____

_____

_____

_____

_____

_____

_____

_____

_____

_____

_____

_____

Gaze into the Mirror of Your Inner Self: What Do You Want That Reflection to Be?

Find Out Who and What *You* Really Are—and Want to Be

Remember the magic mirror in the fairytale *Snow White*? It could not tell a lie. Look in that same magic mirror and ask it, "At the bottom of my soul, magic mirror, at the deepest part of my being, who am I really?" Get beyond the carefully scripted and glibly spoken words. Find that place of thought and reflection where only you go. Then find *you* in that most private of places.

Writing Helps Clarify Deeply Buried Thoughts

Jimmy Carter will be remembered for many things. Many are positive, like the Habitat for Humanity homes he's built and his numerous international peace-keeping efforts. A few are negative, like the failed rescue attempt of American hostages in the Iranian desert. He will also be remembered for authoring one of the best-selling poetry books in the decade, *Always a Reckoning*. Carter uses his poetry to find his inner voice. "I have been able to address inner concerns and doubts and strained relationships through poems that I could never have approached even in my most intimate conversations with my wife. She would read the first draft of a poem and say, 'I never knew you felt this way.' And I said, 'I'm not sure I even knew I felt this way.'"

Thinking about Death Helps Polish the Mirror of Life

"How do you want to be remembered?" the speaker asked from the podium. "Write the eulogy you'd like at your funeral." Her words were followed by lots of scribbling in the crowded auditorium. "Now, is that who you are today?" she asked. "Could some reasonably objective person say those words about you today?" Her words were followed by lots of squirming and shifting in the suddenly uncomfortable seats. She let the silence hang heavy for an eternity or two. Then she leaned into the microphone to be certain that it picked up every nuance of her words and asked, "What are you going to do, starting today, to become the person you just wrote about? Today! Right now!" Think about her questions. They can be both cloth and Windex for that mirror of yours.

Find a Coach to Help You Find *You*

Everybody needs a boost—and a booster. Coaches perform that valuable function. They can help transport you from where you are to where you want to be. You read about coaches in the chapter on the 6th Commandment. Find yourself a coach who can help you transport—and transform—yourself.

> ✿ Neal Lenarsky is the business executives' agent par excellence. He combines the roles of shrink, headhunter, marketer, mentor, and deal maker all in one. "My job is to brand you, keep you branded, and give you exposure." Wow! Sounds like what we all need. But before Lenarsky can take the product called "you" out to the marketplace, he spends days with you to discover who and what you *really* are and want to be. He discovers what you really want in life and in your career; your greatest sources of inspiration and frustration; and your value systems (your feelings about the importance of pay, titles, and relationships with colleagues).

Coaches like Lenarsky help you figure out all the stuff that's not easy to figure out on your own.

Become Your Own Coach and Find *You*: Master the Decide-Practice-Reflect Skill

Coach yourself. Can't be done, you say? Many great players study their own performances in order to improve themselves.

✲ Tony Gywnn, one of baseball's greatest hitters, is a perpetual student of his own performance. He continually studies films of his hitting performance. He *decides* how he wants to swing, *practices* his "new" swing, records it, *studies* it, makes adjustments, and then repeats the cycle. Use Tony's decide-practice-reflect cycle:

- Decide who you want to be and what you want to be doing. Set both short and long-term goals.

- Practice your performance. Play hard. But, pay attention to your performance. Continually read the situation by noticing whether your words and actions are achieving your goals and how other people are responding.

- Reflect on your experience. Now that the game's over, review the game films to find out how you *really* did.

Get Your Actions to Reflect the You That's in Your Heart of Hearts

Align what you do and say with who and what you are. Run the motion camera on yourself. Do your words and actions—both public and private—reflect the *you* you really are? What does that motion picture starring *the real you* tell you about what you do and don't do to "walk your talk"?

Get Feedback from Others

Talk to people and encourage them to help you see *the real you* now and what you want to become. Do some homework first answering the following four questions:

- How would I describe myself now?
- How do I want to be described in three to five years?
- What do I have to do to become who I want to become?
- What help do I need to accomplish my transformation?

With those questions in mind, share your thoughts with anyone who you think can contribute to your insights. Ask them the following five questions:

- How would you describe me now?
- Knowing what you know about me, can I become who I want to become?
- Are my current and future activities going to help me become who I want to become?
- Do I need more or different help than I've identified?
- How can you help me?

The picture sometimes isn't pretty—just real!

Get Straight—Get Real—Be Authentic

Who are you really now? Be honest. No one's picture is ever as pretty or as perfect as they'd like. But deal with reality.

✿ Warren Bennis illustrates authenticity by quoting Robert Bolt's preface to his play, *A Man for All Seasons*:

"Thomas More . . . became for me a man with an adamantine sense of his own self. He knew where he began and left off . . . he located his self. And there . . . [he] set like metal . . . and could no more be budged than a cliff."

APPLICATION

Where are your boundaries? Where do you "begin" and "left off"?

_____

_____

_____

_____

_____

_____

_____

On what issues do you "set like metal" and "like a cliff cannot be budged"?

_____

_____

_____

_____

_____

_____

_____

_____

_____

Build the "We" Community Based upon Mutual, Other-Oriented Commitments

Keep Reminding People about What's Important: Bringing Each Other Fulfillment

Life is a puzzle-assembly task. The puzzle is composed of millions of odd-shaped pieces, there are many people working at the table, and each person has his or her own set of puzzle pieces. The challenge is to assemble the pieces to make a wonderful life for all community members. Your task: Hold high the puzzle picture so everyone can see what we collectively are working to create—and how *their* puzzle pieces fit in.

The puzzle picture itself is this: Help each other become captains of our own fates and masters of our own souls. This is the eternal principle of the Ten Commandments of Success. You do it when you help others grow their captaining and mastering skills. In the process, everyone becomes richer, better, fuller, and more fulfilled human beings.

It's been said that it takes a whole village to raise a child. It takes a whole community to become the captain of your fate and the master of your soul. The collective purpose of life is: Form a community of mutual captains and masters—individuals committed to help each other become better human beings as they work, live, and play together. Covetous thoughts, like the daytime rain in Camelot, are forbidden.

Listen to the Heart-Songs Being Played around You

People are singing their song to you—belting out their heart-felt aspirations and desires. Take the time to listen and pay attention.

> ✿ LeeAnn was a receptionist in a sales office. She wanted to be a salesperson. "Take some classes and we'll consider you," her supervisor told her. LeeAnn signed up and earned a certificate in sales. "I'm ready," she told her supervisor, proudly showing off her framed certificate. After two other salespeople were hired, LeeAnn got the message. She took her certificate off the wall, hung it up at a competing company, and doubled her income. Perhaps her former supervisor was hard of hearing.

Get Everyone on the Same Page, Singing the Same Tune

Align actions across your entire universe so that everyone knows who is doing what, how it contributes to their and everyone else's activities, and when it will be done. Capitalize on that glass house in which you live (recall the 9th Commandment) and get everybody working together, rather than at cross-purposes. Reread the 7th and 9th Commandments for more insight into how to align activities.

Connect at the Heart

The head of one of the armed services asked me to lead an organizational reengineering and redesign program. He wanted to consolidate commands and cut about 42 percent from the operating budget. I told him that I'd love to support his efforts but that I was the wrong person for the job. I said, "These are your people. You have fought together, saved each other from death, moved through the chairs together. You are bonded at the heart with each other. They will listen politely to me. They will die for you. You must sit at the head of the table and insist that they all reach agreement and set up a plan to execute that agreement before you retire."

A pregnant pause hung heavy on the phone. Finally he said, "You know, you're right. I know these people and they know me. It's time we sat down, as professionals and citizens and caring individuals, and do what's right for the country and our service." Right on, General.

Play the "heart card" and it trumps everything else on the table.

Park Your Ego at the Door

Businessman-philosopher Max DePree said that great people "abandon their ego to the talents of others." It takes a very special person to see their joy in other people's achievements, particularly when their name is not attached to the achievement.

The ability to park your ego at the door is perhaps best illustrated by a story about the two greatest prime ministers of England in the nineteenth century. It is said that when you had dinner with William Gladstone, you left convinced that *he* was the most brilliant man on the planet. When you left a dinner with Benjamin Disraeli, you were convinced that *you* were the most brilliant person on the planet. Disraeli possessed that rare quality of parking his ego at the door.

Build the "We" Culture:

- Focus on helping other people become the captains of their fates and the masters of their souls.

- Build heart connections with others that enable everyone to share their "real me."

- All members of the community are better than one member alone—and no one is ever alone.

Epilogue: Some Closing Thoughts

Whew! Mastering and captaining is hard work. And you thought pedaling that bicycle was hard!

The journey through this book has been similar to—though not as perilous as—the Israelites' journey through the desert on their way to the Promised Land. After all, they didn't have bicycles!

It's been fun—and I've learned a lot writing these words. I hope you've learned as much reading them.

The "Cliff Notes" Version

The Ten Commandments of Success speak for themselves. But just in case my turgid writing has confused you, here's the "Cliff Notes" summary:

✸ The *first two commandments* lay out preferred thought patterns, urging you to:

  • follow your followers (1st Commandment)
  • reflect humility by avoiding the distracting idols of hubris, arrogance, and ego (2nd Commandment)

✸ The *next seven commandments* describe actions to take to implement the put-others-first and help-others-grow-to-be-better-people mentalities, which enable you and those around you to become captains of their fates and masters of their souls:

Epilogue

✹

164

- use words to grace and honor others (3rd Commandment)
- take time to learn (4th Commandment)
- honor relationships (5th Commandment)
- take the initiative to help others learn and grow (6th Commandment)
- keep your commitments and help others keep theirs (7th Commandment)
- always deliver your best (8th Commandment)
- match your private being with your public persona (9th Commandment)

✹ The *last commandment* integrates thought, feeling, and action, urging you to:

- build a community of people like yourself dedicated to helping others become the captains of their fates and the masters of their souls (10th Commandment)

Lessons Worth Sharing

The writing and reading (and rereading) of this book leaves me with several overwhelming lessons:

People Matter

In a world of "things" and "technology," the good, the bad, and the best all come down to those wonderful, sometimes maddening, often inscrutable but always lovable people who fill my life. As my wife is fond of saying (and demonstrating): "I collect friends, not things—they are infinitely more valuable."

Faith Counts

In a rapidly changing world, where what worked yesterday doesn't work today and tomorrow is shrouded in dense fog, I

need all the faith I can muster. I need to constantly recon-
nect with:

- my spiritual faith
- my faith in the infallibility of these Ten
Commandments of Success
- my faith in my "family"—my primary, work,
community, and human families
- my faith in the future

Learning Pays

The future belongs to those who learn. I'm a learner first,
second, and third. The universe is my classroom, and you
who share the road with me are my teachers. May I always
have the humility to say, "I don't know," the commitment to
say, "I'll find out," and the friends and supporters to say,
"I'll help you do it."

The Future Is Yours to Have and to Hold If . . .

☼ you care

☼ you believe

☼ you learn

**The best is yet to be,
The rest of life, for which the
first was made.***

*apologies to Robert Browning for misquoting his words.

References

4th Commandment: Always Be a Student
TODD WOODY, "See Jane Shop," *The Industry Standard*, July 9, 1999, pp. 68–82.

5th Commandment: Honor Your Relationships
"Management Brief: Crunch at Chrysler," *The Economist*, November 12th–18th, 1994, pp. 93–94.
EDWARD SUSSMAN, "24 Things to Do before You Die," *Worth*, September 1999, pp. 112–24.

6th Commandment: Be the Instrument for Others' Soul Growth
SUSSMAN, pp. 112–24.

7th Commandment: Keep Your Commitments
"Obituary: Frank Johnson, a Reforming Judge," *The Economist*, August 7, 1999, p. 75.
STEVE WULF, reported by Tom Witkowski, "The Glow from a Fire," *Time*, January 8, 1996, p. 49.
THOMAS TEAL, "The Human Side of Management," *Harvard Business Review*, November–December 1996, pp. 35–44.
MORT MEYERSON, "Everything I Thought I Knew about Leadership Is Wrong," *Fast Company*, April–May 1996, p. 71.

8th Commandment: Always Deliver Your Best
KATE A. KANE, " Are You Hyphen-ated Enough?" *Fast Company*, August–September 1996, p. 30.

9th Commandment: Be an Open Book
JAY FINEGAN, "Pipe Dreams," *Inc.*, August 1994, pp. 64–70.
REED ABELSON, "A Push from the Top Shatters a Glass Ceiling," *The New York Times*, Business Section, August 22, 1999.
DUKE HELFAND, "Sacramento Gets High Marks in School Reform," *Los Angeles Times*, Section 1, August 22, 1999, p. 1.

10th Commandment: Build a Community of People Dedicated to Achieving a Higher Purpose
CHUCK SALTER, "ideas.com," *Wired*, September 1999, pp. 292–307.
SUSSMAN, pp. 112–24.
ROCHELLE GARNER, "Show Me the Stock Options!" *Business 2.0*,
September 1999, pp. 52–54.
WARREN BENNIS, "The End of Leadership," *Organizational Dynamics*,
Fall 1999, pp. 71–80.

Epilogue: Some Closing Thoughts
ROBERT BROWNING, "Rabbi Ben Ezra," in *The Complete Poetic and Dramatic Works of Robert Browning*, ed. Horace E. Scudder (Boston: Houghton Mifflin Company, 1895).

✿